THE FALL

A Matter of Guilt

TWAYNE'S MASTERWORK STUDIES

Robert Lecker, General Editor

THE FALL

A Matter of Guilt

Brian T. Fitch

TWAYNE PUBLISHERS
An Imprint of Simon & Schuster Macmillan
New York

Prentice Hall International
London • Mexico City • New Delhi • Singapore • Sydney • Toronto

Excerpts from *The Fall* by Albert Camus, translated by Justin O'Brien.
Copyright © 1956 by Alfred A. Knopf. Reprinted by permission of the publisher.

Twayne's Masterwork Series No. 133

The Fall: A Matter of Guilt
Brian T. Fitch

Twayne Publishers
An Imprint of Simon & Schuster Macmillan
866 Third Avenue
New York, New York 10022

Library of Congress Cataloging-in-Publication Data

Fitch, Brian T.
    The fall : a matter of guilt / Brian T. Fitch.
        p. cm.—(Twayne's masterwork studies series; no. 133)
    Includes bibliographical references and index.
    ISBN 0-0857-8360-1. —ISBN 0-0857-4452-5 (pbk).
    1. Camus, Albert, 1913–1960. Chute. I. Title. II. Series:
    Twayne's masterwork studies : no. 133
    PQ2605.A3734C534   1994
    843'.914—dc20   94-26130
                                                               CIP

The paper used in this publication meets the minimum requirements of American National Standard for Information Sciences—Permanence of Paper for Printed Library Materials. ANSI Z3948–1984.∞ ™

10 9 8 7 6 5 4 3 2 1 (hc)
10 9 8 7 6 5 4 3 2 1 (pb)

Printed in the United States of America

Contents

Note on the References and Acknowledgments

Quotations from *The Fall* are from the English translation of the French text. The first number in the parentheses after each quotation refers to the English translation of Justin O'Brien for Penguin Books. The second number in the parentheses refers to the current French edition published by Gallimard in the Folio collection. I wish to thank my son Fabrice for his careful critical reading of my initial manuscript.

The present study is the result of over 30 years of work on Camus, punctuated by several attempts to grapple with this most complex of his literary creations. It seeks to do justice to the subtlety of *The Fall* by focusing on the process of the text's reception by the reader.

Chronology: Albert Camus's Life and Works

1913   Albert Camus born 7 November in Modovi, Algeria, the second child of Lucien Auguste Camus, a winery worker whose family had emigrated to Algeria from France in 1871, and Catherine Sintès whose family originated in Majorca.

1914   Father dies from wounds at the Battle of the Marne. Family moves to Algiers, where mother works as cleaning woman.

1918–1923   Attends local primary school where he receives extra coaching from his teacher Louis Germain.

1923–1930   Receives scholarship to attend the Lycée d'Alger.

1928–1930   Plays goalkeeper for the University of Algiers soccer team.

1930   Shows first symptoms of tuberculosis. Leaves home to live with his uncle Gustave Acault, a butcher and anarchist who also lives in Algiers and supports him financially.

1932   Studies in Lettres Supérieures at the Lycée. Among his teachers is Roger Grenier, the philosopher and essayist, who was to become a close friend. Publishes four articles in the review *Sud*.

1933   Joins the antifascist movement Amsterdam-Pleyel.

1933–1935   Receives Licence (B.A.) de Philosophie and Certificat d'Études Littéraires Classiques at University of Algiers.

1934   Marries Simon Hié. Joins the Communist party, from which he later resigned (probably in 1937).

1935   Continues his studies while working for the University Meteorological Department, selling car accessories, and being employed as a ship broker and civil servant. Begins writing autobiographical essays for his first book *L'Envers et l'endroit* (*The Wrong Side and the Right Side*).

1935–1936   Writes Diplôme d'Études Supérieures (master's thesis) on
             Plotinus and Saint Augustine. With friends, takes charge of
             the Maison de la Culture and founds Le Théâtre du Travail,
             for which he writes the play *Révolte dans les Asturies* (*Revolt
             in the Asturias*) in collaboration with three friends. Adapts
             Malraux's *Le Temps du mépris* (*Days of Contempt*) for the
             stage.

1936   Travels to Czechoslovakia, Austria, and Italy. Camus separates
             from his wife. Joins the theatrical company Radio Algiers as
             an actor.

1937   Works as a journalist for *Alger-Républicain* under director
             Pascal Pia. Reports on the main Algerian political trials.
             Unable to take the Agrégation de Philosophie and refuses a
             teaching post in a secondary school because of poor health.
             Writes his first novel, *La Mort heureuse* (*A Happy Death*),
             completed in 1938 (published posthumously without his per-
             mission).

1938   Writes a newspaper review of Sartre's novel *La Nausée*
             (*Nausea*).

1939   Completes writing of *Caligula*. Book of essays, *Noces*
             (*Nuptials*), is published. Undertakes inquiry into living condi-
             tions of the inhabitants of the Kabylia region of Algeria.
             Becomes editor in chief of *Soir-Républicain*. World War II
             breaks out, and Camus seeks to enlist in the army but is reject-
             ed for health reasons.

1940   Marries Francine Faure from Oran. Refuses to accept govern-
             ment censorship of his political opinions. This leads to ban-
             ning of *Soir-Républicain* and impossibility of any further
             employment as a journalist. Leaves Algeria for France, where
             he is taken on by *Paris-Soir* as editorial secretary. In May he
             completes *L'Étranger* (*The Stranger*).

1941   Returns to Oran, where he completes *Le Mythe de Sisyphe*
             (*The Myth of Sisyphus*). Begins working on *La Peste* (*The
             Plague*). Works in the resistance as a clandestine journalist and
             information gatherer.

1942   A renewed bout of tuberculosis obliges him to rest. Allied inva-
             sion of North Africa separates him from wife and family until
             end of war. Publishes *The Stranger*.

1943   Publication of *The Myth of Sisyphus* and the first *Lettre à un
             ami allemand* (*Letter to a German Friend*). Moves to Paris and
             becomes reader for Gallimard.

Chronology

1944	Meets and forms friendship with Sartre. Becomes director of Pascal Pia's newspaper *Combat*. Premiere of *Le Malentendu* (*The Misunderstanding*) receives a mixed reception.
1945	Becomes the father of twins, Jean and Catherine Camus. Premiere of *Caligula* is highly successful. "Remarque sur la révolte" is published.
1946	Visits the United States. Completes writing of *The Plague*. For several months abandons his post as director of *Combat*.
1947	Leaves *Combat*. *The Plague* published to immediate success.
1948	Travels to Algeria. Premiere of *L'État de siège* (*The State of Siege*) opens to unfavorable reviews. *Ni victimes ni bourreaux* (*Neither Victims nor Executioners*) is published.
1949	Journies to South America, which weakens his health. Successfully premieres *Les Justes* (*The Just Assassins*).
1951	Publication of *L'Homme révolté* (*The Rebel*) provokes much controversy.
1952	Travels to Algeria. Replies to unfavorable review of *The Rebel* in Sartre's journal *Les Temps modernes* and breaks off all relations with Sartre. Resigns from UNESCO because of the organization's acceptance of Franco's Spain as member.
1953	Stages his own adaptations of *La Dévotion à la croix* (*The Devotion of the Cross*) and *Les Esprits* (*The Spirits*) at the Festival of Angers.
1954	Withdraws from all political and literary activity, writing nothing for the whole year. Publication of the essays entitled *L'Été* (*Summer*).
1955	Adapts Buzzati's *Un Cas intéressant* (*An Interesting Case*) for the stage. Travels to Greece, where he lectures on the theater. Returns to journalism as a contributor to *L'Express*.
1956	Launches an appeal for a truce in Algeria. Ends his collaboration with *L'Express* in February. Successfully stages his adaptation of Faulkner's *Requiem for a Nun*. Attends meeting in favor of Hungarian uprising. *La Chute* (*The Fall*) published.
1957	*L'Exil et le royaume* (*The Exile and the Kingdom*) and *Réflexions sur la guillotine* (*Reflexions on the Guillotine*) published. Stages adaptation of Lope de Vega's *Chevalier d'Olmédo*. Receives the Nobel Prize for Literature.
1958	Nobel Prize speech *Discours de Suède* is published; also, edition of *The Wrong Side and the Right Side*, with a new preface,

and *Actuelles III*, his essays on the Algerian political situation. In poor health. Journeys to Greece. Buys a house at Lourmarin.

1959   Stages adaptation of Dostoevski's *The Possessed*. Considers taking over direction of a Parisian theater. Encounters difficulty in writing but drafts a part of *Le Premier Homme* (*The First Man*) which was to remain unfinished.

1960   On 4 January, killed in a car crash at Villeblevin, near Montereau, in Michel Gallimard's car.

LITERARY AND
HISTORICAL CONTEXT

1

Historical Context

There is some mystery concerning the writing of Albert Camus's last novel.[1] As of the fall of 1955, Camus had made no mention of such a work, and yet by February of the next year, the novel was virtually complete and by mid-March sent off to the printer (Lottman, 560). One has therefore to assume that the novel came into being during the late months of 1955 and the beginning of 1956.

This was a very difficult time for Camus. His last substantial work, *L'Homme révolté* (*The Rebel*), dated from October 1951. It had been several years in the writing and incorporated almost all his political essays and editorials written since *Le Mythe de Sisyphe* (*The Myth of Sisyphus*). Since its publication, apart from the 1954 volume of lyrical essays, *L'Été* (*Summer*), containing texts written between 1939 and 1953, he had had to content himself as a writer with the task of adapting and rewriting a number of other authors' works for the stage, as he felt incapable of pursuing his own literary production.

His troubles, the magnitude of which it is impossible to exaggerate, arose from the extensive year-long polemic occasioned by the publication of *The Rebel* and, in particular, his bitter quarrel with Jean-Paul Sartre, whose friendship he had enjoyed since their initial

3

meeting in 1944. Having been weakened and undermined by his struggle to complete his philosophical essay *The Rebel* while suffering from ill health, aggravated by a trip to South America in 1949, Camus was deeply affected by the falling-out not only with Sartre but with many of the progressive leftist intellectuals. This was provoked by his uncompromising attack on Stalinism in all its forms and by what his critics considered to be the neglect of history and economic conditions in his discourse on revolution. The praise lavished on his essay by conservatives and anti-Communists of all stripes did not help matters. The very personal attacks on his character clearly disillusioned him and yet struck a sensitive chord, precipitating a crisis in his self-image, which appears to have been responsible for a serious undermining of his literary creativity. Camus felt himself to be the victim of a general lack of understanding. His deteriorating state of health and his concern for the political situation in his native land, Algeria, which was inexorably leading up to the War of Independence, made the years preceding the publication of *La Chute* (*The Fall*) the most somber period of his life.

In December 1951, two months after the publication of *The Rebel*, Camus wrote a letter testifying in favor of the Movement for the Triumph of Democratic Liberties (MTLD) that was to be read out at their trial in Algeria. The following year, he resigned from UNESCO to protest the entry into that organization of Franco's Spain, a regime against which he had fought for many years. In 1953 he gave a speech in support of the uprising in East Germany that had taken place on 7 June. His fortieth birthday, 7 November, was a psychological turning point for him, as it is for so many others. His productions of his own adaptation of two plays, *La Dévotion à la croix* (*The Devotion of the Cross*) and *Les Esprits* (*The Spirits*), were followed, in 1954, by a period in which he wrote nothing at all. Moreover, with the exception of his intervention in favor of seven Tunisians who had been sentenced to death, he abstained from any further political activity. In November began the Algerian War, which was finally to lead to the country's independence in July 1962.

Before moving on to this crucial event, we should note that during 1953 Camus was writing what was to be his most autobiographical work, the short story "Jonas," which recounts the trials and tribulations of a painter whose artistic creativity and productivity are victims of his own success, a success as much social as artistic. The demands on his time brought about by his newfound notoriety are such that before long he no longer has either the time or the physical and mental space in which to work on his art. Jonas's fate clearly reflects the predicament his creator found himself in, with neither the necessary time nor, very often, the inclination to pursue his writing and about which he complained bitterly to many of his friends and acquaintances.

Meanwhile, the Algerian War pitted the Algerian nationalists not only against the French government, for whom Algeria was considered not just a French colony but an integral part of France, but also against the Algerian-born children of former European settlers known as *pieds-noirs* (black-feet). These events were experienced as a personal tragedy by Camus, torn, as he was, between his love of justice and his concern for the safety of his family and friends and their right to continue to live in the land of their birth. It was a war marked by bloody atrocities committed by both sides. The conflict appeared to defy peaceful solution by even the most well intentioned, such as Camus, who was better prepared than most to appreciate the opposing points of view, since, as a journalist during the years preceding World War II, Camus fought tirelessly for the political and economic rights of those Arabs who had fallen foul of the French government in Algeria.

In 1955, Camus returned to journalism when given the opportunity to contribute on a regular basis to the Parisian weekly *L'Express*. In January of the next year, Camus made his most determined effort to intervene politically in the Algerian conflict. He returned to Algiers to participate in the Appeal for a Civil Truce, which he was instrumental in launching, having devoted an article to the project in *L'Express*. Its objective, while admittedly limited in scope, was crucial in Camus's eyes: it called for an end to all attacks on the civilian population of both sides. Its thrust was thus humanitarian rather than political; it sought to limit the pointless suffering of the innocent in the midst of a civil war.

This initiative was probably the most important of his interventions in public life and was certainly the one with the potential to have had the most far-reaching political consequences. It was especially significant in that Camus had been constantly criticized by the opponents of the French regime in Algeria for not having taken a clear-cut stand in favor of Algeria's independence from France. To have done so would, in his eyes, have been tantamount to condemning to exile his own community of *pieds-noirs* and thus depriving them of what many considered to be their birthright. As Camus himself put it, "I believe in justice, but I shall defend my mother above justice" (Lottman, 607). The events surrounding the Appeal took place after Camus wrote the first draft but before he completed the final version of *The Fall* (Lottman, 566).

One of the groups in Algiers that was attempting to bridge the ever-widening gap between the French and Arab communities was the Association of Friends of Theater in the Arab Language, which included members of the small minority of *pied-noir* liberals, as well as a few of Camus's friends. They approached Camus to solicit his support. In the article he contributed to *L'Express* on 1 November 1955, Camus suggested that the two sides agree to do everything in their power to spare the civilian population further suffering. This would be the author's position for the rest of the Algerian crisis. In response to the request for support, he flew to Algiers on 18 January 1956 for preliminary discussions to organize the public meeting at which the Appeal was to be launched. Camus was unaware at the time that the Arab members of the Committee for a Civil Truce were key figures in the Front de Liberation National (FLN), the Arab nationalist movement that was the instigator of the uprising against the French, and that the Committee was, in fact, a front for their organization. Unlike Camus, the FLN had no illusions about the inevitable failure of such an initiative, which they hoped would convince the French Algerians that violence was the sole means to obtain justice. One of the Arabs, Mohamed Lebjaoui, did inform Camus before the public meeting, having sworn him to an oath of secrecy, that he belonged to the FLN, and once Camus had gotten over his surprise, he expressed satisfaction with talking directly to a member of that movement.

The meeting took place on the evening of Sunday, 22 January, in a very threatening atmosphere in a building on the edge of the Arab quarter. Security was in the hands of a large number of FLN militants, and the square outside was filled to capacity with thousands of Arabs to contain the counterdemonstration by the *pied-noir* ultras with their cries of "Camus to the gallows." A tense Camus rapidly read his speech, after which the meeting immediately broke up. The next morning only one of the Algerian daily newspapers, *Le Journal d'Alger*, printed his speech in its entirety. Nothing was to come of all this; Camus's Appeal was to fall on deaf ears as far as the French government was concerned. From this point on, Camus refused to take any public political position that might be construed as support for terrorism of any kind.

In May, *The Fall* was published.

2

The Importance of the Work

The Fall is not by any means the most popular of Camus's works. There is no doubt, however, that Camus is better known for his fiction than for his plays or his essays. Of his novels and short stories, *The Stranger* and *The Plague* have been much more widely read. This does not mean that his last novel is not widely known but merely that most readers probably come to it only after they have already discovered his other two novels. That this should be so is hardly surprising, for it is not an easy work to read. In comparison, *The Plague*, partly because of its allegorical meaning as a depiction of France under the German Occupation during World War II, makes for a more immediately satisfying reading experience, and *The Stranger*, with the lyrical writing that characterizes the climaxes coming at the end of both parts of the novel, more than compensates the reader for the uneasiness that Meursault's narrative initially arouses.

Clamence's tale is far more disconcerting, and its ending, unlike those of the previous two novels, provides no resolution of the problems posed by what has gone before, no satisfying psychological release for its reader. On the contrary, by the end of the book, the reader remains acutely aware of a dilemma with no resolution in view. Moreover, whether or not the reader is already familiar with Camus's writings makes little difference. Indeed, at the time of its publication, those who knew and appreciated his work and all that its creator had come to stand for were the most disturbed by their discovery of his latest novel. Few knew what to make of such a troubling and puzzling work.

The perplexity that the novel provoked in its readers is a measure of its importance within the Camusian canon. In a manner similar to Jean-Paul Sartre's autobiographical work *Les Mots* (*The Words*), Camus's novel puts in question all of the author's previous works, recasting them in a new light;[1] and as the author was to die only four years after its publication, it effectively punctuates the closing years of his career with a question mark.[2] There is no doubt that this is Camus's most complex and enigmatic literary production and, I contend, his most successful creation. The fact that it comes at what was to be the culminating point of his career is, of course, no coincidence, for what more fitting moment could there be for him to bring to fruition his art as a novelist? That its writing was no doubt as satisfyingly cathartic for its author as its reading is deeply unsettling for the reader is not the least paradox of this paradoxical work.

I will briefly compare *The Fall* with his most famous novel, *The Stranger*, which, coincidentally, has introduced nonfrancophone students across five continents to the French language, a socioliterary phenomenon without precedent. Elsewhere,[3] I have attempted to show how the extraordinary impact that *The Stranger* has had on generations of readers around the world is achieved in spite of the structural problems revealed by a close study of the text, not to mention the degree to which it taxes the reader's credulity both by its caricatural portrayal of the French legal system and by calling on him or her to believe that a jury of *pied-noirs* would in any circumstances—let alone in those depicted—sentence one of their fellows to death for the killing of an Arab. It is, in reality, two novels very skillfully rolled into one, without the reader becoming aware of the fact: its first part corresponds to a twentieth-century version of the French naturalist novel and its second part to a rewrite of the romantic novel, here pitting not an artistic genius but a "hero" in spite of himself, banal to the point of anonymity, against the malevolent forces of an uncomprehending society. In contrast, the text of *The Fall* bears the closest critical scrutiny without revealing any such anomalies: form and content here come together to constitute an aesthetically perfect whole, as satisfying on subsequent readings as on the first. Out of the most disparate elements—the horrors of totalitarianism, a society of suspicion and moral uncertainty, the trials and tribulations of professional success, the incipient personal tragedy of a writer at the end of his tether confronted by the prospect of creative sterility—Camus has crafted an object of literary perfection. Out of what was perceived (perhaps rightly so, but who can say?) as human failure emerges artistic success: his chef d'oeuvre. That is no coincidence either, for the writer placed in the crucible of his literary creativity the innermost core of his being, his most vulnerable self.

Camus's work has rightly been seen to be characterized by understatement and the closely contained expression of emotion one associates with classical art. *The Fall* is an obvious exception to this; indeed, one could go so far as to say that it luxuriates in overstatement. Here, his reader has to make appropriate allowance not for what is left unsaid, or at best understated, but for what is clearly exaggerated to the point of caricature. The distinction is between having to read more into what one is reading, or less. The latter activity is perhaps more demanding, or at least calls for more subtle and judicious discrimination on the part of the reader, than the former. In *The Fall*, the least "classical" of his novels, Camus has succeeded in surpassing the finely honed skills of the author of *The Stranger* and *The Plague*. There is something about this particular text that suggests that the literary work somehow went beyond the immediate reach and the studied control of its creator—not, it must be stressed, in the sense that it says more than he intended to say but, on the contrary, in that this, his most personal creation, attains a universality characteristic of only the greatest of literary works.

One of the paradoxes of Camus's literary output is that in spite of his love for the theater and his ongoing activity as actor, director, dramatist, and adapter of other writers' novels for the stage, his own plays did not enjoy great success. Given *The Fall*'s formal affinities with the dramatic monologue, the character of Jean-Baptiste Clamence could well be considered the finest dramatic role Camus ever created. Eloquent proof of this is found in the recording of his own reading of its first chapter.[4]

3

Critical Reception

There is probably no other modern writer who has had more written about him during his own lifetime than Albert Camus, and since his death, the writing of articles, monographs, books, and theses dealing with his work has continued unabated. More of this ever-increasing body of criticism has been devoted to Camus's fiction than to any other part of his literary output. While there are fewer books and critical writings on *The Fall* than on *The Stranger*, one of the most widely read and frequently translated novels of the twentieth century, Camus's last novel has received considerably more critical attention than either *The Plague* or the short stories of *The Exile and the Kingdom*. The work's complexity, its formal ambiguity and originality, and the many features that sharply distinguish it from the author's previous works suffice to explain the attention it has continued to receive from the critics. To date, no less than nine monographs or books have been devoted to this novel (five in French, three in English, and one in German), not to mention chapters in the several hundred books on Camus and many dozens of articles.

When *The Fall* was published in May 1956, Camus's readers had long been awaiting the appearance of a major new work since the publication of his philosophical essay *The Rebel* in 1951. His preceding novel, *The Plague*, dated from 1947. Consequently, the appearance of this, his first major work since his controversial essay, which had met with such criticism as to give rise to a year-long polemic, was the object of considerable curiosity on the part of readers. And their curiosity was, to say the least, not disappointed. In fact, it would have been difficult to conceive of a more disconcerting work coming from the pen of the Franco-Algerian writer who had devoted so much of his fiction and nonfiction to the land of his birth and the milieu of his youth, situated on the shores of the Mediterranean. When it appeared, this work immediately posed a problem of interpretation: before its readers could attempt to understand how the author had come to write such a strange story, resembling nothing that he had ever written before, they had to decide what it meant, what its author was trying to say to them. There can be no doubt that the reading public had great difficulty in deciding what to make of Clamence's monologue, shot through, as it clearly was, with heavy irony that called out to be deciphered and yet appeared to defy interpretation in any definitive form.

Those critics who reviewed *The Fall* when it appeared were particularly struck by the work's ambiguity, not only with regard to the content of Clamence's monologue but also with regard to its form and structure. Although it was formally designated a *récit* (a unilinearly structured short novel-form)[1], it had attributes in common with other literary genres such as the allegory, the essay, the *conte moral* or philosophical tale, the satire, the prose poem, and the Russian *skaz* (a short novel narrated in the first or third person that depicts the world of the protagonist in his own particular language). Others were equally struck by its moral ambiguity and attentive to its religious overtones, seeing in it a changed attitude toward Christianity, one that might even herald the author's future religious conversion. Those who believed the judge-penitent to be speaking for the author diagnosed his discourse as symptomatic of someone suffering from a state of severe depression exacerbated by acute narcissism. Gaëtan Picon was one of the first to make the connection between this text and the polemic concerning *The Rebel*, a line of inquiry that was to be pursued by a number of critics over the years.[2]

Given the difficulty of determining to which literary genre *The Fall* belonged since it bore more resemblance to a dramatic monologue than to a novel, it appeared natural to seek out any possible literary antecedents. Dostoevski's *Notes from Underground*, André Gide's *Paludes* (*Marshlands*), and Arthur Rimbaud's *Une Saison en enfer* (*A Season in Hell*) were among the first to be "identified," and they were soon followed by many others. The work was so unusual that it incited the critics to ever greater efforts to seek out possible sources. The paradoxical outcome was to be that more sources would come to be claimed for *The Fall* than had been attributed to any other of the author's works. Apart from the most obvious influences, such as Dante's *The Divine Comedy*, Lermontov's *A Hero of Our Time*, Buzzati's *Un Cas intéressant* (*A Clinical Case*), and the Bible, later candidates to be singled out were Dostoevski's *The Possessed*, *The Double*, *The Dream of a Ridiculous Man*, and the Grand Inquisitor episode in *The Brothers Karamazov*; Joseph Conrad's *Lord Jim*; Luigi Pirandello's *Non si sa come* (*One Doesn't Know How*); Duhamel's *La Confession de minuit* (*Confession at Midnight*); René-Louis des Forêts's *Le Bavard* (*The Gossip*); Julien Green's *Épaves* (*Wreckage*); Jean Lorrain's *Monsieur de Bougrelon*; Baudelaire's "L'Invitation au voyage" ("An Invitation to Voyage") and *De l'essence du rire* (*The Essence of Laughter*); Franz Kafka's *The Trial*; Hugo's *Le Dernier Jour d'un condamné à mort* (*The Last Day of a Condemned Man*); Montherlant's *Les Jeunes Filles* (*The Girls*); Diderot's *Le Paradoxe sur le comédien* (*The Paradox of Acting*) and *Le Neveu de Rameau* (*Rameau's Nephew*); and Friedrich Nietzsche's *Human, Too Human*. Paradoxically, the result of this seemingly insatiable search for sources—an activity largely discredited in contemporary literary studies—has been to bring home to us the remarkable originality of Camus's last novel.

Camus's death on 4 January 1960 led to the publication of a number of commemorative issues of literary journals such as *La Nouvelle Revue française*, *La Table ronde*, and *Preuves* and an outpouring of articles and essays. The most significant of these was Roger Quilliot's "Un Monde ambigu" (first published in *Preuves*), since he was in a position to draw on unpublished documents, a personal acquaintance with Camus, and an extensive knowledge of political life.

He was able to identify the novel as an indirect confession and a cry from the author's heart. This article was subsequently integrated into the second edition of his important study of Camus's works, entitled *La Mer et les prisons* (*The Sea and Prisons*, originally published in 1956). In 1962 he was to present and annotate the first volume of the Pléiade edition of Camus's collected works, *Théâtre, récits, nouvelles* (*Theater, Narrative, Stories*); the second volume, *Essais* (*Essays*), followed in 1965. The publication of the collected works, together with the considerable documentation it made available, put subsequent research on a sounder footing and enabled Camusian studies to develop in earnest.

The first study to be devoted to the structure and the meaning of *The Fall* was authored by Adele King and published in 1962; King provided a remarkably concise and satisfying account of the work.[3] A number of critics sought to situate *The Fall* in relation to the rest of Camus's work, especially in relation to *The Stranger*. The most felicitous of these studies was René Girard's "Camus' *Stranger* Retried"; for Girard, *The Fall* originated in the defective structure of *The Stranger*, which he saw as the objective projection of the author's *mauvaise foi* or insincerity. Using a broader autobiographical context, Conor Cruise O'Brien, in an original and controversial political reading of the work, maintained that the novel had its roots in the Algerian problem and that Clamence's moral crisis was none other than the dilemma its creator faced, torn between, on the one hand, his concern for justice for his Arab compatriots and, on the other, his love for his mother and his allegiance to his fellow *pieds-noirs*.[4] The character of the protagonist, Clamence, in all its ambiguity, continued to attract the attention of the critics, who understandably found much to occupy them, given the obsessive nature of his insistent monologue.

The publication of Carina Gadourek's important study of Camus's whole literary production in 1963 launched a new line of inquiry: the character and role of Clamence's interlocutor.[5] She was the first critic to attempt to reconstruct the missing half of the dialogue. Overall, Gadourek's chapter on *The Fall* was the most thorough and systematic of aesthetically oriented studies of the novel to date and remains one of the best accounts of the work in that it does justice to the complexity of the work. Five years later, H. Allen Whartenby was to pursue the same enterprise even more thoroughly and recreate all of the interlocutor's verbal responses and reactions only to arrive at a conclusion opposite to that of Gadourek, holding that Clamence's companion remains wholly unconvinced by the judge-penitent's pseudo-confession.[6] Thus, methodological concerns began to be voiced as critics sought to set aside authorial intention, changing the focus of scholarly inquiry away from the confusion of Clamence with his creator in favor of an aesthetic appreciation of the novel's form and technique.

A new emphasis began to manifest itself as critics of a psychoanalytic bent began to address themselves to the judge-penitent's monologue. Following the stress placed by certain critics on the obsessive character of Clamence's monologue, a more systematic study of his psychological makeup was undertaken in 1968 by José Barchilon,[7] followed a year later by Michael A. Sperber's reading of the novel in light of the Icarus complex,[8] a complex that brings together many of his personality traits, such as his narcissism, ascensionism combined with the prospect of falling, a craving for immortality (reascension), and a conception of woman as an object to be used for narcissistic gain. It was not until 1973, however, that a book-length psychoanalytic study of the whole of Camus's work was published.[9] Those of a more aesthetic bent had to await the publication of Jean Gassin's study in 1981 to discover a psychoanalytic account of the whole of the author's writings sufficiently sophisticated to take into account the aesthetic and methodological concerns of the literary critic.[10]

The year 1970 saw the publication of the first book to be devoted entirely to *The Fall*, by Pierre-Louis Rey,[11] and of a collective volume of studies on the work.[12] That year, the first International Conference on Camus convened.[13] Rey's book, although brief and in a schematized pedagogical format, constituted a serious, well-researched, and well-balanced presentation of the novel that gave some account of its complexity without, however, its many judicious insights being organized to provide an analytical account of the text and its overall structure. The volume in the Albert Camus series of *La Revue des lettres modernes* published four studies by established Camus scholars and reviewed all the published research on *The Fall*. Two of the studies, by Roger Quilliot[14] and myself[15] stress the theatricality of the work with regard to Clamence's masklike role and to the actual fictional space evoked not only by his assumed character but also by his sheer bodily presence. The other two deal with language: the first, by Jacqueline Lévi-Valensi,[16] shows how the novel reveals the treacherous nature of language, constituting an allegory of language itself, and the second, by André Abbou,[17] provides one of the first linguistic analyses of the text. The Camus 1970 conference included the first study to be devoted to the imagery of *The Fall*, in this case the imagery of falling implied by the title.[18]

The linguistic approach to the text was subsequently pursued by Marten Nøjgaard in a long article that provided the most detailed study of the form and structure of the novel to date;[19] finally, in 1977, a book-length linguistic study by Claudine and Michel Maillard appeared.[20] Elsewhere, the linguistic concepts of the *locuteur* (the speaker), the *délocuteur* (what is spoken about), and the *allocutaire* (the addressee) were also called upon to unravel the two-tiered communicative chain operative in the novel, the first involving Sartre and Francis Jeanson and the second *The Fall*'s other readers.[21]

The Maillards' book was preceded, three years earlier, by the second book to be devoted solely to *The Fall*, a study by Phan Thi Ngoc-Mai and Pierre Nguyen Van-Huy.[22] This study gave the most detailed analysis of Clamence's psychological makeup undertaken so far, seeing in him a pathological case of megalomania and persecution complex. Explicitly informed by a theological and Christian reading of the text, it insisted on the satanic side of his character.[23] The novel's Christian imagery and its many biblical resonances had already been studied by earlier critics.[24]

Several scholars have examined the religious dimension of the novel by focusing on the role of Hubert van Eyck's painting *The Adoration of the Lamb*. The latter was examined at some length by Jeffrey Meyers[25] to reveal the manner in which the message of the painting provides an ironic contrast to the godless theology of the novel and by Phillip H. Rhein to show how it serves to blend the biblical world of John the Baptist with the twentieth-century bourgeois world of Clamence.[26] Subsequently, Jean Gassin's psychoanalytic interpretation of the painting, presented at the important Albert Camus 1980 conference in Gainesville, Florida, saw it as providing a commentary on the main themes of all of Camus's works.[27]

The next monograph-length study of the novel, by Yves Reuter, introduced a new dimension to understanding *The Fall* by undertaking an ideological reading of the text.[28] Camus's text was seen to disrupt ideological discourse by putting in question the codes corresponding to sociocultural values and shifting interest away from the product (the fiction) to the process (the production of the fiction). It is true that a few years earlier, another critic, François Zumbiehl, writing in a rather inaccessible Hungarian academic journal, had sown the seeds for such a reading by analyzing the work as a pastiche of literary discourse and of the ideal of the seventeenth-century *honnête homme*.[29] Reuter was to provide a full-fledged and concise study of the ideological dimension of the text that highlighted the reasons why critics found it so difficult to classify either in relation to the rest of Camus's work or in relation to the recognized literary genres, and why the standard French textbooks of literary history therefore barely mentioned it, despite the many pages devoted to Camus's literary production. Little, if any, notice had previously been taken by the critics of the manuals' omitting to comment on *The Fall*, and yet once attention was drawn to the fact, their omission was clearly seen to be as significant as it was surprising and indicative of the text's subversive potential.

In 1980 a critical guide to both *The Stranger* and *The Fall* was published by Rosemarie Jones. She approached *The Fall* through the significance of its title and the various roles Clamence plays; she then moved to a consideration of its structure and its form and style.[30] Her well-informed study, brief and concise, contains many revealing insights. Interestingly, by comparing the two novels, Jones was led "to see in *La Chute* Camus's major work of fiction" (91), an opinion with which I concur.

Mention should also be made of the pages devoted to *The Fall* in David Ellison's *Understanding Camus*, published ten years later, for without constituting a study of the novel, they provide many perceptive critical comments.[31]

The 1985 publication of Alex Argyros's *Crimes of Narration: Camus' "La Chute"* confirmed the interest, already obvious from Reuter's study, in reading Camus's text in light of contemporary literary theory.[32] While Reuter had recourse to Louis Althusser's treatment of ideology, Argyros called upon the writings of Jacques Derrida, as well as on Sigmund Freud and Martin Heidegger. He insisted on maintaining a rigorously formal approach, treating the text as an artifact, scrupulously respecting the fictional status of the work and its protagonist, and refuting the idea of the existence in the text of a multilayered meaning. For him, literature was flat, all surface. The result was a highly original reading of *The Fall*. Others, for their part, drew upon Mikhail Bakhtin,[33] Gérard Genette,[34] and the hermeneutics of Hans-Georg Gadamer[35] and Paul Ricoeur.[36]

The self-referential character of Camus's text also emerged for the first time as it was seen to be emblematic of the very process of the reading[37] and the appropriation[38] of the literary work. In other words, "there is a self-reflexive dimension in *La Chute* that is not merely autobiographical but textual," as David Ellison points out in an important study[39] in which he draws on Maurice Blanchot's challenging 1971 reading[40] of the novel to reveal "its potential for the elaboration of a theory of interpretation" (27). This most recent turn in studies devoted to Camus's last novel has served to show that in spite of the author's undoubtedly classical bent as a writer of prose fiction, responsible for works clearly taking their place in the French literary tradition, *The Fall* is also a text in the contemporary sense of the term[41] with all its undecidability. Thus it is that it has much to contribute to the contemporary debates in literary theory and properly belongs to the intellectual climate of our time, to what the French refer to as *la modernité*.

A READING

4

Camus and *The Fall*

The relationship between Camus and his last novel is complex and subtle. Indeed, it would be difficult to conceive of a more complex series of motives than those that went into the writing of *The Fall*, motives that were no doubt in no small part responsible for the complexities of this most difficult and intriguing work. Although the vast majority of literary works lend themselves to what has become, since the advent of New Criticism and, more recently, French Poetics, the predominant manner of studying literary works, that is, considering them as autonomous formal entities, it is not, in my opinion, possible to ignore the autobiographical dimension of *The Fall* without emasculating the work and failing to do justice to the irony that permeates it.

Camus conceived this novel, which was originally intended to take the form of a short story to be included in the collection entitled *The Exile and the Kingdom*, during what was without a doubt the most difficult period of his whole existence. It can be stated unequivocally that had it not been for his bitter quarrel with Sartre in 1952, Camus would never have written *The Fall*, and his readers would have been deprived of his most challenging literary creation. Let us examine the context in which it came to be conceived.

From the late 1930s onward, Camus and Sartre had recognized in each other a kindred spirit, as is witnessed not only by Sartre's famous review of *The Stranger* but also by Camus's earlier review of Sartre's first novel, *Nausea*. They shared the same left-wing nonconformism common to so many French writers and intellectuals and were both not only novelists and dramatists but also the authors of philosophical essays. Even if Camus did not lay claim to the same professional credentials as Sartre as a philosopher, he had devoted his Diplôme d'Études Supérieures (the equivalent of the master's thesis) to Plotinus and Saint Augustine. Moreover, his early writings shared with Sartre's the existentialist sense of the absurd. There could be no doubt in either of their minds that they were in the same ideological camp. Nevertheless, their affinities did not mask fundamental differences of temperament and character: the sensual North African enamored of the sand and the sea was worlds apart from the cerebral Parisian intellectual.

When the 1951 publication of his second philosophical essay, *The Rebel*, received a markedly hostile reception, without precedent in his career as a writer, Camus was clearly taken aback by the virulence of the criticisms aimed at his essay by left-wing writers. The fact that Sartre's journal led the attacks with a scathing review by Sartre's close collaborator Francis Jeanson did not sit well with Camus. He responded with a vigorous defense of his work, published in the same journal, only to provoke in addition to a response from Jeanson a highly critical article from Sartre, who felt that he himself (rather than Jeanson) had been the real, undeclared target of Camus's attack in his original letter. Sartre went so far as to attack both Camus's essay and his character.

The preliminary exchange was bitter, and both sides were unyielding in their attacks. Camus was clearly upset by their falling-out. He felt deeply wounded, given his respect for Sartre, and their quarrel left scars that would be long to heal. So long, in fact, that Camus went through a number of frustrating years during which his creative inspiration dried up completely and he fell back on the writing of theatrical adaptations, such as those of Dostoevski's *The Possessed* and William Faulkner's *Requiem for a Nun*. It was clear that many of Sartre's criticisms, not only of *The Rebel* but also of Camus's character, had struck home, provoking in Camus a personal crisis of debilitating self-doubt. Indeed, if the scars ever did heal—and we cannot be sure, because of his premature death only four years after the publication of *The Fall* in 1956 and the disappearance of his personal diary at the time of his death—it can only have been thanks to the writing of Clamence's tale, which, in that it clearly reflects a process of relentless and pitiless self-questioning on the part of its author, must have fulfilled for him a therapeutic function.

Although Clamence's grating cynicism is in striking contrast to the humanistic optimism of *The Plague*, the informed reader soon recognizes a number of troubling similarities between the Amsterdam lawyer and his creator. Camus, too, was "of respectable but humble birth" (23; 33). His father, unlike Clamence's, who was an officer, was merely an ordinary soldier conscripted to fight in World War I, in which he lost his life. Clamence remarks upon his own physical resemblance to a football player (9), and we recall that Camus was goalkeeper of the football team at the University of Algiers. Even Camus's theatrical activities as an actor—if not his profession of dramatist and director—are not altogether foreign to Clamence, who during his internment in a prisoner-of-war camp played out the role of the pope; indeed, he mentions that his visiting card reads, "Jean-Baptiste Clamence, play-actor" (36; 52).

Clamence's résumé of his own attributes is even more strikingly applicable to his creator: "I was accceptable in appearance; I revealed myself to be both a tireless dancer and an unobtrusively learned man; I managed to love simultaneously—and this is not easy—women and justice; I indulged in sports and the fine arts" (22; 32). This description brings to mind not only the photo found in Jean-Claude Brisville's book on Camus of the author appearing to dance as he directs his actors in a rehearsal for one of his plays[1] but also his reputation in Parisian circles for being something of a Don Juan, just like Clamence, who would "have given ten conversations with Einstein for a first meeting with a pretty chorus-girl" and who confesses: "How often, standing on the pavement involved in a passionate discussion with friends, I lost the thread of the argument being developed because a devastating woman was crossing the street at that very moment" (45; 65). And it is easy to imagine Camus's lifelong love of sports and of everything associated with the theater prompting the following remark: "I have never been really sincere and enthusiastic except when I used to indulge in sports and, in the army, when I used to act in plays we put on for our own amusement" (65; 93).

Above all, the hedonistic sensualism of the author of the lyrical essays gathered under the title *Nuptials* is reflected in Clamence's whole attitude to life: "Yes, few creatures were more natural than I. I was altogether in harmony with life, fitting into it from top to bottom without rejecting any of its ironies, its grandeur, or its servitude. In particular the flesh, matter, the physical in short, which disconcerts or discourages so many men in love or in solitude, without enslaving me, brought me steady joys. I was made to have a body" (22–23; 32). Here we find expressed the same love of life, the same delight in the pleasures afforded by the senses, and the same feeling of corporal well-being.

The judge-penitent's life before his "fall" was one unending success, success that was, moreover, taken for granted, as though it were somehow his birthright: "As a result of being showered with blessings, I felt, I hesitate to admit, marked out. Personally marked out, among all, for that long and uninterrupted success" (23; 33). It is interesting to note that in 1958, responding to a questionnaire submitted to him by an American scholar,[2] Camus confessed to being conscious of dwelling under his own particular star, which, as he stated in *Carnets* (*Notebooks*)[3] eight years previously, he had always followed instinctively (*Carnets*, 303). And when Clamence declares that "without desire, women bored me beyond all expectation" (75; 108), he appears to be echoing Camus's equally misogynistic remark that "outside love, women are boring" (*Carnets*, 27).

It is, however, important to bear in mind that all the aforementioned attributes pertaining to the narrator-protagonist of *The Fall* and the life he leads apply to his past life, before the incident on the bridge when he failed to respond to the young girl's cry for help and the subsequent revelation he experienced with regard to the true nature of the life he had led until then. When Clamence begins to question this all-too-flattering portrait of himself, he discovers a self that was the product of systematic self-deception, and this realization motivates his pseudoconfession. That being so, where exactly does that leave Camus in relation to the judge-penitent's pitiless and all-encompassing self-condemnation? This is what tempts the knowledgeable reader to see in Clamence's tale a kind of personal confession or mea culpa on the part of its author, however indirect that "confession" may be, given the fictional genre in which it is couched. After all, Sartre and his friends made precisely that assumption, as we learn from the memoirs of Sartre's lifelong companion, Simone de Beauvoir.[4]

In fact, the more knowledgeable the reader is with regard to the rest of Camus's work, the more tempted he will be to subscribe to such an autobiographical reading of *The Fall*. Clamence's life before his fall echoes that of Tarrou in *The Plague*: "When I was young I lived with the idea of my innocence: that is to say, with no idea at all. . . . I brought off everything I set my hand to, I moved at ease in the field of the intellect, I got on excellently with women and, if I had occasional qualms, they passed as lightly as they came. Then one day I started thinking. And now . . ." (201; 222). One can even identify references to Camus's career as a writer, for the author of *The Stranger* might well be commenting on his role in writing that novel when Clamence remarks, "Not only did I run no risk of joining the criminal camp . . . , but I even took up their defence, on the sole condition that they should be noble murderers, just as others are noble savages" (16; 23). What is perhaps the most remarkable aspect of that earlier novel is the fact that it takes as its hero an "innocent" murderer, that is, someone who is clearly responsible for the death of another and yet of whose complete innocence the author seeks to persuade us, siding with his character in the most flagrant manner in the second part of the novel. This has led one critic not only to see the end of *The Fall* as possibly being "an ironical allusion to the concluding pages of *The Stranger*" but also to go so far as to maintain that "in a curious way, *The Fall* appears to be a studied rewriting of *The Stranger*" (Ellison, 149, 162). The author of *The Stranger* certainly subscribed to what Clamence calls his "instinctive scorn for judges" (15; 22). "I could not understand," he explains, "how a man could set himself up to perform such a surprising function" (16; 22). A similar lack of understanding gave rise to the caricatural portrait of the judge in the second part of *The Stranger*.

And yet Clamence is himself a self-professed judge, even if he also claims to be a penitent. Having satirized the figure of the judge in his first novel and then treated him with distinctly more compassion in portraying the character of Judge Orthon in *The Plague*, Camus now takes a judge for the sole protagonist of what was to be his last novel. This choice of character is surprising in light of his very negative view of the legal system in general—a view characteristic of French left-wing intellectuals in general, it is fair to say. It is true that by profession, Clamence is not a judge but a lawyer. But then lawyers were depicted in no more sympathetic a light in *The Stranger* than was the judge. For the reader familiar with the author's previous works, there cannot fail to be something distinctly disconcerting about Camus's choice of hero.

I have still not exhausted all the autobiographical resonances in this work. Those that remain will likely escape the notice of the majority of readers. They are expressions and turns of phrase that echo the quarrel between Camus and Sartre acted out in the pages of Sartre's journal *Les Temps modernes* in August 1952. It is these allusions that go a long way toward helping us grasp the true tenor of the autobiographical level of meaning in *The Fall*. There are, moreover, explicit pointers to the uncomfortable situation in which Camus found himself as a result of that bitter polemic, as when Clamence remarks, "For a long time I had lived in the illusion of a general agreement, whereas, from all sides, judgements, arrows, mockeries rained upon me, inattentive and smiling. . . . I received all the wounds at the same time and lost my strength all at once" (59–60; 85), or when he says, "May heaven protect us, *cher* monsieur, from being set on a pedestal by our friends!" (25; 36).

In his response to Camus's letter concerning the review-article of *The Rebel*, Francis Jeanson wrote, "You sound, moreover, like a person who is enamoured of his solitude, with the pride and arrogance that goes with it,"[5] just as Clamence confesses, "In solitude and when fatigued, one is inclined, after all, to take oneself for a prophet" (86;

123). Jeanson saw Camus as "that great voice soaring above the factions,"[6] and Clamence takes up the very same image when he exclaims, "Then, soaring over this whole continent which is under my sway without knowing it . . . , I am happy" (105; 152). In his response to Camus's letter to Jeanson, Sartre chided him with the remark, "Good Heavens! Camus, how *serious* you are and, to use one of your expressions, how frivolous you are!"[7]—a reproach that Clamence appears to echo, as though confirming the original accusation: "To be sure, I occasionally pretended to take life seriously. But very soon the frivolity of seriousness struck me" (64; 92). Likewise, Clamence's observation that "each of us insists on being innocent at all costs, even if he has to accuse the whole human race and heaven itself" (60; 86) appears to substantiate Sartre's reproach: "In order to placate your conscience, you have to condemn, someone has to be guilty: if it isn't you, then it will be the whole world."[8] The almost identical phrasing found in the novel and Sartre's and Jeanson's texts in *Les Temps modernes* cannot possibly be coincidental. Here, too, there is a process of rewriting at work that is at the source of all the other rewriting involved in *The Fall*—not only that of *The Stranger* and *The Plague* but also that of *The Rebel*.

Finally, Camus referred to the famous Parisian cafés frequented by Sartre and his friends, those "special cafés where our professional humanitarian free-thinkers gathered" (68; 98), as Clamence puts it, existentialism being associated for the general public with the café life of Saint-Germaìn-des-Près. There is, too, an ironic allusion to Sartre's publishing of the memoirs of a prostitute in his journal *Les Temps modernes* when Clamence evokes the prostitute who, in his words, "has since consented to write her memoirs for a confessional paper quite open to modern ideas" (77; 110–11).

The verbal echos of the quarrel with Sartre clearly take on an ironic resonance in the text and confirm the lasting effect of their falling-out on the author. It is not merely that Camus is quoting almost literally his adversaries' words but that in putting them into the mouth of a fictional character who bears a certain resemblance to himself, he appears to be capitulating to his critics. It is as though Camus were somehow seeing himself through their eyes. Is it possible then that the creation of the fictional Clamence constitutes a recognition of the truth of the accusations leveled against him? Had Camus subsequently become convinced by his critics? To believe as much would be to mistake a work of fiction for autobiography.

In order to take the present discussion one significant and, indeed, decisive stage further, it is necessary to take a look at certain existentialist themes of the work that contribute to its philosophical dimension. Camus's earlier work shared with Sartre's the existentialist themes associated with the absurd,[9] and the same holds true for *The Fall*. Indeed, here such themes come even more sharply into focus than in the novel that preceded it, *The Plague*. Existentialism—a philosophical tendency (rather than a body of thought) that has its origins in the writings of the Danish theologian Søren Kierkegaard and of the German philosopher Friedrich Nietzsche—has as one of its first principles that man's existence precedes his essence; that is, before *being* anything in particular, man has to *act* on the basis of free personal choice. This means that man has no ready-made identity arising from some kind of innate human nature; on the contrary, his identity is always provisional, the result of the sum total of his actions up to a given point in time, and provisional until the moment of his death, when his identity becomes fixed and immutable. This first principle of existentialism is clearly articulated when Clamence remarks, "One could not die without having confessed all one's lies. . . . Otherwise, even if there were only one lie hidden in a life, death made it definitive" (66; 95). While he is alive, man can enjoy no certain, clearly definable identity; by bringing an end to life, death confers on man an identity: "Men are never convinced of your reasons, of your sincerity . . . except by your death. So long as you are alive, your case is doubtful" (55; 79). The theme of man's immutability after death is reiterated when Clamence says that "the ideal solution would have been the death of the person I was interested in. Her death would . . . have fixed our relationship once and for all" (50; 72). (I might add here that Sartre's famous play *Huis clos* [*No Exit*] constitutes a dramatic illustration of the point.)

For the existentialist, as for Clamence, there is nothing more terrible than the freedom (of choice) of Man without God and the anguish inevitably and inescapably arising therefrom: "At the end of all freedom is a court sentence; that's why freedom is too heavy to bear. . . . Ah, *mon cher,* for anyone who is alone, without God and without a master, the weight of days is dreadful" (97–98; 141). Finally, virtually all social life, characterized, as it necessarily is, by habit and codified behavior, is seen by the existentialist to be inauthentic, inasmuch as it invariably takes the form of role-playing. This is precisely the way Clamence views his past life as a Parisian lawyer when he speaks of "playing [his] role as well as [he] could": "I played at being efficient, intelligent, virtuous, a good citizen, shocked, indulgent, responsible, high-minded . . ." (64; 92–93).

The existentialist tenor of Clamence's discourse would appear at first sight to confirm a transparently autobiographical reading of *The Fall.* If this tale seems to put in question the author of *The Stranger,* does it not at the same time represent a turning back from the uplifting humanism of *The Plague* and *The Rebel* to an earlier, existentialist philosophy seen by so many readers to be exemplified in Camus's first novel and expounded in *The Myth of Sisyphus?* Upon closer examination, it soon becomes apparent that the existentialist themes in question have much more in common with Sartre's writings than with Camus's early works. Central to the Sartrean form of existentialism is the concept of the other person who subjects us to his judgment: "God is not needed to create guilt or to punish. Our fellow men suffice. . . . You were speaking of the Last Judgement. . . . I have known what is worse, the judgement of men" (81; 117). Beneath his unrelenting gaze, we become reduced to objects, and nothing is more unbearable than to see ourselves reduced solely to what we are for others (our being-for-others, as Sartre put it): "If everyone . . . displayed his true profession and identity . . . ! Just fancy visiting-cards: Dupont, jittery philosopher, or Christian landowner, or adulterous humanist. . . . But it would be hell! Yes, hell must be like that: streets filled with shop-signs and no way of explaining oneself. One is classified once and for all" (36; 52). Although for Sartre, "hell is other people," Camus's previous writings manifest no sense whatsoever of the other person being perceived as a constant threat. When Clamence remarks, "I don't know how to name the odd feeling that comes over me. Isn't it shame, perhaps?" (51; 74), one recalls that in Sartre's famous philosophical work *L'Être et le néant* (*Being and Nothingness*), it is man's sense of shame that proves to him the existence of others. Thus, it is difficult to mistake Clamence's existentialist pronouncements for Camus's earlier philosophy of the absurd.

Moreover, even the uninformed reader cannot fail to perceive the heavy irony with which these existentialist themes are often evoked, as in the case of the concept of commitment: "I lived my own life under a double code, and my most serious acts were often the ones in which I was the least involved" (65; 94). Even more blatant is the scathing reference to the theme of freedom: "Once upon a time, I was always talking of freedom. At breakfast I used to spread it on my toast, I used to chew it all day long. . . . With that keyword I would bludgeon whoever contradicted me" (97; 140). This heavy and insistent irony can alert even the reader with no knowledge of the author's earlier quarrel with Sartre that something more is going on here than meets the eye, for it is difficult to attribute this relentless irony, which exerts a caricatural effect on its object, solely to Clamence and his rejection of his past life. It cannot fail to suggest to the reader that the author, too, is distancing himself from the existentialist ideas previously espoused by his character: Clamence before his fall is not, in this respect, to be identified with the early Camus.

The existentialist echoes are thus to be seen, paradoxically, as an integral and inevitable part not of the way in which Camus saw himself but, on the contrary, of the way he was seen by Sartre. For Sartre, too many similarities and affinities existed between Camus's searly writings and his own, as was pointed out earlier, for him not to tend to read his own ideas into Camus's texts, as could be seen from his review of Camus's first novel.[10] In other words, an element of parody here enters into the picture: among many other things, *The Fall* is also a parody of Sartrean existentialism, and Clamence's unenviable fate makes of this work a kind of cautionary tale pointing out the dangers of the Sartrean form of existentialism (very much in the way that Sartre's own short story "L'Enfance d'un chef" ["The Childhood of a Leader"] constitutes a morality tale of existentialist inauthenticity).

To appreciate the true autobiographical dimension of this work in all its remarkable complexity, one must understand that Clamence is indeed a portrait of its author but a portrait with a difference since here, paradoxically, Camus is seen through Sartre's eyes. What we have is a conscious self-caricature, inspired by the accusations leveled at its creator by his critics. *The Fall* is Camus's final and considered response to those critics, a response that takes the form of a riposte, for it sets a trap into which many were to fall (witness Simone de Beauvoir's account of the novel in *La Force de l'âge* [*The Prime of Life*]). For those particular readers and for them alone, Camus intended his work to be taken as a confession right up until the final pages, when Clamence's explanation of the true motivation underlying his recounting of his past life would reveal their mistake. This was his way of getting back at them, leading them to see in the character a portrait of its author and subsequently turning the tables by revealing the apparent self-portrait to be but a caricature, and a gross one at that. In this way, Camus the artist prevails over his critics, whereas Camus the polemicist was hard put to get the better of Sartre in the pages of *Les Temps modernes*. And nothing could be more appropriate, for it is precisely in the realm of literary creativity in general and in his fiction in particular that Camus excels.

This being so, should *The Fall* not be placed in the category of what the French refer to as *littérature de circonstance*, that is, a work only intelligible within the context of the very specific circumstances in which it was written and hence liable to become dated for later readers when those circumstances have been completely forgotten? The answer, fortunately, is no, for if that were the case, Camus's novel would not be seen as the masterpiece it is. In fact, *The Fall* is no less effective, its impact is no less great, for the reader who has no knowledge of Camus's life or the rest of his work and has merely picked the book up at random from the library shelf. Herein lies what is no doubt its most remarkable attribute: the way in which this work addresses both a specific reader (that is, Sartre and his friends) and just any reader (Fitch, 1976).

In conceiving such an intricate and elaborate work as *The Fall*, Camus found a way of pursuing, and perhaps laying to rest, his inner demons without offering himself up as a sacrificial victim to his critics. For nothing could have been further from his mind than to increase his vulnerability, of which he was only too painfully aware, and in the process, substantiate their allegations. His sensitivity, often manifested in his relations with others, dictated the turning of a confession into an accusation that represents both a strategy of self-defense and an indication that he had perhaps finally managed to come to terms with himself. Indeed, how else could he have come to write such a work?

5

The Two Worlds of *The Fall*

In literary studies it is customary to speak of the world of a given novel, for every novel embodies a universe in which its characters live out the story that is told. The world in question is, of course, a fictional world, a creation of the writer's imagination, and will be brought to life by the reader's imagination. In between times—after the novel has been written and before it has been read—that world exists in a latent form within the text of the novel, waiting to take on form and substance in the mind's eye of the reader. The fact that the novelistic universe is an imaginary world does not, however, prevent it from being situated geographically in a very precise manner. Such is the case of *The Fall*, in which the events recounted take place in two cities of whose real-life existence there can be no doubt—Amsterdam and Paris.

What is peculiar to this particular novel of Camus's is that there are not one but two worlds in *The Fall*, and they correspond to the two cities. However, it is not merely because Amsterdam and Paris are situated at some distance from each other, in two different countries, that one is led to speak of two worlds rather than one. Within the novel, the Dutch and French cities are separated not only in space but also in time: Amsterdam belongs to the present and Paris to the past, and neither one encroaches on the time frame of the other. In other words, Clamence tells his story in Amsterdam, but he lived the events that make up his story in Paris. This is, however, not the only reason for drawing a clear distinction between the two different worlds, as we shall see later when we come to examine the implications of Clamence's revelation at the end of the novel. Let us begin by looking at the depiction of the Dutch capital city.

The novel opens with the characters situated in a bar called Mexico City, the haunt of sailors and shady characters of all kinds, Amsterdam being, of course, an international port. The scene is not set immediately at the beginning of the first chapter, and the first depiction of the characters' surroundings takes the form of the haunting sound of "the fog-horns in the harbour," which occasions Clamence's remark that "there'll be fog tonight on the Zuyderzee" (10; 14). In fact, the subsequent evocation of the city is decidedly atmospheric and claustrophobic, with its "crowd of people swarming on the pavements, wedged into a little space of houses and canals, hemmed in by fogs, cold lands, and the sea steaming like wet washing" (11; 17). The Dutch are characterized by "their heavy tread on the damp pavement" and their moving "ponderously in and out of their shops full of gilded herrings and jewels the colour of dead leaves," their heads in a "fog compounded of neon, gin, and peppermint emanating from the red and green shop-signs above them" (12; 17). The red and green colors soon give way completely to the color of dead leaves, which, by association, evoke falling[1] autumnal leaves, already prefigured by the very title of the novel (Jones, 50–62): "Holland is a dream, Monsieur, a dream of gold and smoke—smokier by day, more gilded by night. And night and day that dream is peopled with Lohengrins like these, dreamily riding their black bicycles with high handle-bars, funeral swans constantly drifting throughout the whole country, around the seas, along the canals. Their heads in their copper-coloured clouds, they dream; they ride in circles; they pray, sleep-walking in the fog's gilded incense" (12; 17–18). In short, they are at one and the same time "here and elsewhere" (11; 17), elsewhere being the exotic climes of Holland's colonial dependencies: "They have gone thousands of miles away, towards Java, the distant isle. They pray to those grimacing gods of Indonesia with which they have decorated all their shop-windows and which at this moment are floating aimlessly above us before alighting, like gorgeous monkeys, on the signs and stepped roofs" (12; 17–18). This wonderfully evocative description, one of the very few visually powerful passages in all of Camus's fictional writings, has much the same effect on the reader as a painting. The whole scene is suffused with the merging of gold-tinted light and swirling fog to create a harmonious blending of its parts. At the same time, the language has a haunting, poetic quality about it. There is every reason to believe that in writing this passage and even more so in penning the equally poetic and ironic evocation of the sexual license associated with this international port city that brings the first chapter to a close, the author had in his mind's eye the exotic imagery of a famous poem by the nineteenth-century French poet Charles Baudelaire, "L'Invitation au voyage" ("An Invitation to Voyage"). The second of these passages reads, "What? Those ladies behind those windows? Dream, Monsieur, cheap dream, a trip to the Indies! Those persons perfume themselves with spices. You go in, they draw the curtains and the navigation begins. The gods come down onto the naked bodies and the islands are set adrift, lost souls crowned with the tousled hair of palm trees in the wind. Try it" (13–14; 20).

Amsterdam's most striking characteristic is its canals, described in this miniature tableau: "Amsterdam asleep in the white night, the dark jade canals under the little snow-covered bridges, the empty streets, my muffled steps . . ." (106; 153). They furnish the occasion for an oblique reference to another literary work, Dante's *The Divine Comedy*: "Have you noticed," asks Clamence, "that Amsterdam's concentric canals resemble the circles of hell? . . . Here, we are in the last circle. The circle of the . . . Ah, you know that?" (13; 18–19). It is, above all, a waterlogged city characterized by "the breath of stagnant waters, the smell of dead leaves soaking in the canal" (34; 48) and "the silhouettes of boats in the fog" (13; 19). Everywhere there is what Clamence refers to as "this damned humidity" (82; 118). All is flat and colorless because of the incessant fog in this "the most beautiful negative landscape": "Just see on the left that pile of ashes they call a dune here, the grey dyke on the left, the livid beach at our feet and, in front of us, the sea looking like a weak lye-solution with the vast sky reflecting the colourless water. . . . Everything horizontal, no relief; space is colourless and life dead" (54; 77–8). Adding to the pervasive grayness is the sky of Holland, "filled with millions of doves . . . which flap their wings . . . , filling the heavenly space with dense multitudes of greyish feathers . . ." (54; 78). It would be difficult to conceive of a world more different from the sunbathed North African landscape of Camus's other novels and short stories than this "desert of stones, fogs and stagnant waters" (86; 24).

As for the bar Mexico City, where Clamence begins his conversation with his interlocutor, it is never described. Just like his room ("bare . . . but clean. A Vermeer, without furniture or copper pots" [88; 128]), the setting for the final chapter, its presence is implied but never explicitly depicted. The reader is nonetheless brought back unfailingly to the Dutch setting at the beginning and (with the exception of chapter 5) the end of each of the intermediary chapters, which are taken up entirely by Clamence's story of his past, Parisian life, and is never allowed to lose sight of the world of the narrator and his listener, a fact that will prove to be of significance to the outcome of the novel.

The gray melancholy of the Dutch port, with its swirling fog diffusing any source of light or color, in which all is suffused with a dank and oppressive humidity, creates a distinctly claustrophobic effect. Moreover, there can be felt to be something threatening in that all that can be made out are vague shapes and human figures barely glimpsed in the all-pervading gloom where people "vainly try to make out the silhouettes of boats in the fog" (13; 19). It is the kind of place in which anything could happen, the potential setting for dark and mysterious happenings. At one point, Clamence remarks, "Look, the doves are gathering up there. They are crowding against one another, hardly stirring, and the light is waning," adding ominously, "Don't you think we should keep silent to enjoy this rather sinister moment" (70; 101–2). In short, it creates in the reader a sense of foreboding, which, by the end of the novel, will prove to have been only too well founded.

In the other world of *The Fall*, the Parisian environment in which Clamence practiced his profession as a lawyer, the material reality of the city plays considerably less of a role than it does in Amsterdam and its surrounding landscape. Here the world is portrayed in terms of the society that inhabits it; place gives way to the people who live there. The Parisians could have been depicted just as the Dutch landscapes and cityscapes are, but in fact, little is learned about their appearance. Instead, Clamence's comments focus on the way they behave. A sociological dimension is thereby introduced into the novel with a quite detailed account of how that society functions and of the lifestyle of its inhabitants.

It is true that the setting on the quays of the Left Bank of the Seine, near the Pont des Arts, where Clamence, on "a fine autumn evening, still warm in town and already damp over the Seine," hears the sound of laughter, is described briefly with "the street-lamps . . . glowing dimly" and "the river . . . gleaming between the stalls of the second-hand booksellers" and "dusty leaves that still recalled summer" (29; 42). A similar setting near the Pont Royal is evoked just as briefly as the backcloth to the later fateful incident on the bridge, when Clamence fails to go to the aid of the young woman who has thrown herself into the river: "It was an hour past midnight, a fine rain was falling, a drizzle rather, that scattered the few people on the streets" (52; 75). Finally, there is a moment, near the end of the novel, when Clamence recalls to mind the beauty of the city he has left behind: "Evening falls, dry and rasping, over the roofs blue with smoke, the city rumbles, the river seems to flow backwards" (87; 125). More often, however, Paris's tangible presence, its material reality, is reduced to "a real *trompe l'œil*, a magnificent dummy setting inhabited by four million silhouettes" (7; 10). The description of its inhabitants as mere silhouettes gives the reader a foretaste of the scathing indictment of contemporary society that is to come.

It is a society in which "avidity . . . is a substitute for ambition" (17; 24) and "spitefulness . . . a national institution" (8, 12). It is organized so as to achieve the "liquidation" of the individual, just like "those tiny fish in the rivers of Brazil that attack the unwary swimmer by thousands and with swift little nibbles clean him up in a few min-

utes, leaving only an immaculate skeleton" (8; 11). This is achieved by
the integration of the individual into preordained social structures that
swallow him live so that he, as an individual, disappears without trace:
"'Do you want a good clean life? Like everybody else?' You say yes,
of course. . . . 'O.K. You'll be cleaned up. Here's a job, a family, and
organized leisure.' And the little teeth attack the flesh, right down to
the bone" (8; 11–12). As Clamence puts it, later on in the novel,
"bourgeois marriage has put our country into slippers and will soon
lead it to the gates of death" (78; 112).

Particular Parisian types also appear, such as the "café atheists"
when Clamence refers to "the special cafés where our professional
humanitarian free-thinkers gathered" (68; 98) and the left-wing intellectuals, ever ready to "launch two or three manifestoes, maybe even
more" (34; 49), at the slightest provocation. Their depiction is invariably satirical, if not straightforwardly sarcastic, as in the case of those
he calls "our moral philosophers," "so serious, loving their neighbours
and all the rest—nothing distinguishes them from Christians, except
that they don't preach in churches" (98; 142).

Society as depicted is based on a pecking order: everyone has
somebody below him in the hierarchy in order to be able to satisfy his
or her need to dominate, for "everyman needs slaves as he needs fresh
air," as Clamence explains: "The lowest man in the social scale still has
his wife or his child. If he's unmarried, a dog" (34–35; 49–50).

It is a materialistic world in which "all strive to be rich," the reason being that "wealth shields from immediate judgement, takes you
out of the subway crowd to enclose you in a chromium-plated auto-
mobile, isolates you in huge protected lawns, Pullman cars, first-class
cabins" (61; 87). It is also a world in which everyone is only too happy
to judge his neighbour, being "as ready to judge as . . . to fornicate."
As proof of his claim, Clamence cites "the table-conversation during
August in those summer hotels where our charitable fellow-citizens
take their cure for boredom." And he adds tellingly, "Observe your
own family; you will learn a thing or two" (57; 82). The judgment of
our fellows proves to be even more formidable than the Last Judgment
itself, so that "God is not needed to create guilt or to punish"—"our
fellow-men suffice" (81; 117). "Let's not give them any pretext," says

Clamence, "no matter how small, for judging us. Otherwise, we'll be left in shreds" (57–58; 82).

All social behavior is portrayed as a form of playacting. For Clamence, the difference between the world of the courtroom, where he earned his living as a lawyer, assuming the identity of his clients in order to plead their case before the jury, and the everyday world is minimal: "Notice your neighbours if perchance a death takes place in the building. They were asleep in their little routine and suddenly, for example, the concierge dies. At once they awake, bestir themselves, get the details, commiserate. A newly dead man and the show begins at last. They need tragedy, don't you know; it's like their little transcendence, their apéritif" (27; 38). People need to have a part to play and therewith a sense of identity and the impression of fulfilling a function in the overall social scheme of things. He comments that all he saw around him seemed to him to be "merely an amusing game" (64; 92), wholly lacking in any significant import. In short, nothing in the social affairs of humans is worthy of being taken seriously, for there is little difference between the games people play and the roles people act out.

It would be difficult to conceive of a more negative and pessimistic depiction of society than the one presented in *The Fall*. Social life and its organization appear to lack any redeeming features whatsoever. Clamence's account of the lifestyle of his contemporaries is shot through with an unrelenting cynicism.

Many features attributed to this society are not restricted to Parisian or even French society but are characteristic of Western society in general, including, of course, Holland. It is precisely because the Parisian world in which the past events he recounts took place is depicted not so much as a geographical place but as a social setting, the mere backdrop to a way of life, that it ends up taking on a greater generality and being less clearly circumscribed than the world of Amsterdam, in which Clamence is situated as narrator. The sociological dimension of the novel thus tends to spread out from the specific world of the practicing lawyer Clamence to encompass the whole of contemporary society so that the distinction made earlier between the world of Amsterdam and that of Paris becomes blurred: "Power . . . settles everything. . . . Our old Europe at last philosophizes in the right way" (35, 50). In some respects, the Parisian is representative of nothing less than modern man himself. And when Clamence comments scathingly, "It always seemed to me that our fellow-citizens had two passions: ideas and fornication," he is quick to add, "Still, let us take care not to condemn them; they are not the only ones, for all Europe is in the same boat" (7; 10).

It is only on this sociological level, however, that the two worlds become interchangeable, and then only to a limited extent. Clamence points out, for example, that "with these people [the Dutch, in contradistinction to the French], at least, spitefulness is not a national institution" (8; 12). For the reader, the two worlds do remain distinct, primarily because one belongs to the present and the other to the past. But another distinguishing factor is the form in which each is evoked: the haunting and troubling mists of the Amsterdam canals run not the slightest danger of being confused with the comedy of Parisian society.

6

Clamence the Protagonist:
The Parisian Lawyer

The Fall is a novel narrated in the first person, but it is a first-person narrative with a difference. In the case of most narratives where the narrator and the protagonist are one and the same person, the present time in which the narration takes place is very clearly subordinated to the past time in which the events related occurred. Caught up by the story told, the reader often loses sight of the narrator, having become immersed in the world of the past. In *The Fall*, however, the narrator is very much a character in his own right at the same time as he is fulfilling his role of narrator. Although there is not a single word in this novel for which Clamence is not directly and solely responsible—in other words, everything which the reader is led to picture in his mind's eye is conjured up by Clamence's own words and his alone—his function as a narrator never eclipses his physical presence as a character, existing side by side with the man with whom he first strikes up a conversation in the Amsterdam bar. It therefore appears more appropriate to refer to the judge-penitent as a storyteller rather than a narrator, in spite of the fact that it is his own words that bring the storyteller to life before he sets out to recount his past Parisian existence. Just as I made a clear distinction between the two worlds of this novel, it is necessary to distinguish no less clearly between Clamence the judge-penitent and Clamence the lawyer. In this chapter, I shall begin by studying the character of the Parisian lawyer.

The story of Clamence's past life is punctuated by three crucial events. The first is recounted in chapter 2, where Clamence, while standing on the Pont des Arts, is suddenly startled by the sound of laughter coming from somewhere behind him, but when he turns around, the source is nowhere to be seen (30; 43). The second is recounted in chapter 3 and takes place on the same bridge when Clamence passes by a young woman leaning over the railing and looking into the river below; a moment later, he hears a body striking the water, followed by "a cry, repeated several times . . . going downstream," which then "abruptly ceased" (52; 75). He hesitates for a moment before going on his way. The third event is related in chapter 5 and occurs during a trip on an ocean liner when he spots "a black speck on the steel-grey ocean" (79; 114) and at once averts his gaze. When he looks again, the speck has disappeared. Thinking that it was someone drowning, he is on the point of calling out for help, only to catch sight of it once again and to realize that it is, in fact, a piece of floating debris. This is a moment of veritable illumination for him, and he does not fail to draw from it the appropriate conclusions: "Then I realized, calmly, just as you resign yourself to an idea the truth of which you have long known, that that cry which had sounded over the Seine behind me years before had never ceased, carried by the river to the waters of the Channel, to travel throughout the world, across the limitless expanse of the Ocean, and that it had waited for me there until the day I encountered it. I realized likewise that it would continue to await me on seas and rivers, everywhere, in short, where lies the bitter water of my baptism" (80; 114–15).

The reference to his baptismal water conjures the religious imagery that runs throughout the novel, beginning with the title's allusion to the biblical fall of Adam. This realization marks Clamence's entry into a new life, and the new life in question will culminate in a change of profession from lawyer to judge-penitent. The young woman's falling into the river marks, then, in a very real albeit nonreligious sense, Clamence's fall from grace. This is, it should be stressed, a fall from grace in his own eyes and in his own eyes alone. It brings about a transformation in his conception and hence opinion of himself. But let us begin by examining the person he was before his fall from grace.

Clamence was a person who had attained the height of success in his chosen profession and the pinnacle of self-satisfaction—in short, what many would consider happiness in the fullest sense of the term. Professionally, he was a most successful, well-known lawyer, highly esteemed by his colleagues, and his skills were fully appreciated by his grateful clients:

> Being stopped in the corridor of the law-courts by the wife of a defendant you represented for the sake of justice or pity alone—I mean without charging a fee—hearing that woman whisper that nothing, no, nothing could ever repay what you had done for them, replying that it was quite natural, that anyone would have done as much, even offering some financial help to tide over the bad days ahead, then—in order to cut the effusions short and preserve their proper resonance—kissing the hand of a poor woman and breaking away—believe me, *cher* Monsieur, this is achieving more than the vulgar ambitious man and rising to that supreme summit where virtue is its own reward. (19; 27–28)

He had, moreover, the satisfaction of specializing in what he refers to as "noble cases," those in defense of "the widow and the orphan" (15; 21). As he puts it, "You really might have thought that justice slept with me every night." Clamence was admired for "the accuracy of [his] tone, the appropriateness of [his] emotion, the persuasion and warmth, the restrained indignation of [his] speeches before the court" (15; 22). In his professional life, he was, in short, "beyond reproach" (17; 22), never accepting bribes or cultivating journalists. In fact, his qualities received public recognition when he was awarded the Légion d'Honneur, which he was able to decline with what he calls "a discreet dignity" (17; 24), that is, without any self-serving ostentation, virtue being its own reward, as it were.

As for his personal life, it was no less a source of satisfaction to him. His popularity knew no bounds, and he enjoyed constant social success. He was equally at ease with women and with participating in sports or indulging his love of the fine arts. He sums up his situation thus: "Just imagine, I beg you, a man at the height of his powers, in perfect health, generously gifted, skilled in bodily exercises as in those of the mind, neither rich nor poor, sleeping well and fundamentally pleased with himself without showing this otherwise than by a happy sociability" (22; 32). Self-satisfaction was clearly the key to his state of mind and his attitude toward life. His whole existence was perceived by him as forming a harmonious whole: he was at one with himself, instinctively in accord with life in general and his own existence in particular. And it was not only socially that he felt so much at ease but also physically, experiencing, as he did, a perfect corporal equilibrium, with no excess of any kind.

What is more, although he is of humble birth, he felt that this extraordinary state of affairs was only to be expected, as though it were his birthright. In other words, he considered that he had some kind of divine right to the success and happiness that was his. He believed that "as a result of being showered with blessings," he was "personally marked out, among all, for that long and uninterrupted success" (23; 33) and that his "happiness was authorized by some higher decree" (23; 34), notwithstanding the fact that he had no religious belief in any higher being.

Thus, he found himself at a summit of human success and happiness that could not, he felt, be excelled. And, indeed, he had a distinct predilection for heights of any kind. "Yes, I have never felt comfortable except in lofty surroundings," he tells us. "Even in the details of daily life, I needed to feel *above*. . . . A natural balcony fifteen hundred feet above a sea still visible bathed in sunlight was . . . the place where I could breathe most freely" (19–20; 28–29).[1] But when he adds, "Especially if I were alone, well above the human ants," the reader probably already suspects the flaw in his character. Moreover, there is something suspect, something that does not quite ring true, in his all too systematic enumeration of the high vantage points he seeks: "I preferred the bus to the underground, open carriages to taxis, terraces to being indoors. I was an amateur pilot in planes in which one's head is in the open. While on boats I was the eternal pacer of the top deck. In the mountains I used to flee the deep valleys for the passes and plateaux . . . Coal-bunkers, ship-holds, subways, grottoes, pits were repulsive to me" (19–20; 28). It is clear that, potentially at least, he has a long way to fall, and fall he does, as a result of the three crucial incidents in his life.

When he returns home on the evening on which he had heard the sound of laughter behind him, he encounters something very strange as he looks into his bathroom mirror: "My reflection was smiling in the mirror, but it seemed to me that my smile was double . . ." (31; 44). This impression is in striking contrast to his experience up until that moment. Now, something suddenly comes between him and the image he presents to the world in his everyday life, something that destroys the sense of complete harmony that has been at the core of his existence.

Now, a sense of harmony is the key to any impression of being sincere. Sincerity entails our feeling that there is not the slightest discrepancy between our beliefs, opinions, and principles, on the one hand, and our words and deeds, on the other hand. Standing in front of the mirror, Clamence experiences a disconcerting discrepancy between how he feels himself to be and how he appears from the outside to other people. This leads him, before long, to identify with the image of "a double face, a charming Janus" (36; 52). Later, I shall return to the theme of the double, which is central to understanding Clamence's character and his subsequent evolution.

In light of these three incidents, Clamence begins to question his satisfaction with himself and the life he has been leading. Once he begins to examine his existence, he soon comes to the realization that he has been living under an illusion, and a monumental one at that: "My dream had not stood up to facts. I had dreamed—this was now clear—of being a complete man who managed to make himself respected in his person as well as in his profession. Half Cerdan, half de Gaulle, if you will" (41; 59–60). "Just from being so fully and simply a man, I looked upon myself as something of a superman" (23; 33). Far from being the "complete man" he had taken himself for, he discovers that every detail of the portrait of himself that he had nurtured and cherished is irremediably flawed: "I realized, as a result of delving in my memory, that modesty helped me to shine, humility to conquer, and virtue to oppress. . . . Thus the surface of all my virtues had a less imposing reverse side" (62–63; 90). And thus the portrait is turned inside out, as though a photograph had become its corresponding negative, white exchanged for black and black for white. I shall come back later to the perfect symmetry of this reversal.

For example, what he took to be his innate modesty turns out to be nothing of the sort: "I have to admit it humbly, *mon cher compatriote*, I was always bursting with vanity. I, I, I is the refrain of my whole life and it could be heard in everything I said. I could never speak without boasting . . ." (37; 53). As for his professional life, he finally realizes that he "was on the side of the guilty, the accused, only exactly in so far as their crime caused [him] no harm." "After that," as he says, "it is very hard to continue seriously believing one has a vocation for justice and is the predestined defender of the widow and orphan" (42; 61). On the contrary, whenever he felt threatened, he was even more merciless than the judge himself, wanting to "strike down the offender and get him on his knees" (42; 61).

What he is led to undertake through this reevaluation of his past behavior is nothing less than a complete reassessment of the life he has led. This is most clearly revealed by his recounting the satisfaction he derives from helping blind men across the road. This habit of his is first described in these terms: "I loved to help blind people cross streets. From as far away as I could see a cane hesitating on the edge of a pavement, I would rush forward, sometimes only a second ahead of another charitable hand already outstretched, snatch the blind person from any solicitude but mine, and lead him gently but firmly over the pedestrian crossing amidst the hazards of the traffic towards the quiet haven of the other pavement, where we would separate with a mutual emotion" (17; 25). Subsequently, he views this behavior in quite a different light: "I discovered something. Whenever I left a blind man on the pavement to which I had convoyed him, I used to touch my hat to him. Obviously the hat-touching wasn't intended for him since he couldn't see it. To whom was it addressed? To the public. After playing my part, I would take my bow. Not bad, eh?" (36–37; 52–53).

As far as his relations with women are concerned, it becomes clear to him that "sensuality alone dominated [his] love-life" ("an infirmity that was," as he points out, "convenient") and that "even for a ten-minute adventure [he]'d have disowned father and mother" (44; 63–64). In fact, he has come to recognize in himself "a congenital inability to see in love anything but the physical." This unbridled sensuality, he now discovers, overrides all the fine principles he had thought to hold, making him an exemplary hypocrite: "I had principles, to be sure, such as that the wife of a friend is sacred. But I simply ceased quite sincerely, a few days before, to feel any friendship for the husband" (44; 64).

Having previously interpreted his actions in a manner that could not have reflected more favorably on him, Clamence now sets about attributing to himself a wholly different motivation, which puts quite another complexion on them. This systematic revision of the past image that he presented to himself and took pleasure in assiduously cultivating results in a fundamental reinterpretation of his past life. Similarly, the reader of *The Fall*, like the reader of any novel, interprets, of necessity, while reading, for interpretation is inseparable from the process of reading. I shall return later to the consequences to be drawn from this situation where Clamence is taking part in the same activity that the reader is involved in,[2] so that the reader may very well be made aware of his or her own role as interpreter and of all it entails of a judgmental nature once he or she realizes that what is involved is an interpretation of an interpretation.

Clamence discovers these facts, which he refers to as "truths," about himself only "little by little" (37; 54). But once he is alerted to what he believes to be the true nature of the motivation underlying his whole existence, he soon discovers that the whole coherent and satisfying portrait of himself that he has built up over the years begins to unravel: "For a long time I had lived in the illusion of a general agreement, whereas, from all sides, judgements, mockeries rained upon me, inattentive and smiling." He adds, "The day I was alerted I became lucid" (59–60; 85). Once anyone begins to question what he had previously taken for granted, doubt sets in and spreads relentlessly until nothing whatsoever of his past certainties is left standing. The process, once in motion, takes on its own inner momentum, steamrolling everything in its path. For example, "Once my attention was aroused," he remarks, "it was not hard for me to discover that I had enemies" (58–59; 84). And indeed, the moment he sets out to bring to light motives that he suspects to have remained hidden up to that point in time, he inevitably finds them, for is it not true that people always manage to find, sooner or later, what they are looking for?

The point to make here is that the results of Clamence's soul-searching are inevitable—they are part and parcel of the process itself—and that anybody who indulges in such an activity arrives at the same conclusions. Once sincerity is questioned, it will invariably be found wanting, if only for the fact that sincerity is a quality that can only be ascribed to someone else whose actions we can readily compare with their stated principles. What self-scrutiny reveals is, by its very nature and of necessity, far too formless, imprecise, and unclear to compare with the tangible and verifiable conduct of our everyday existence, the reflection of which is to be seen in the eyes of those around us.

Moreover, the systematic soul-searching Clamence is led to undertake entails introspection, a process whereby one attempts to turn in upon oneself in order to see into one's innermost thoughts and feelings. Introspection is a form of self-scrutiny that always calls for a kind of "doubling-up" of oneself, so that one becomes both the subject doing the scrutinizing and the object of that scrutiny. By definition, therefore, those who indulge in introspection cannot feel at one with—that is, in harmony with—themselves. Likewise, Clamence, as he begins to examine the person who had lived out his life up to that point in time, can no longer enjoy the impression of being "altogether in harmony with life, fitting into it from top to bottom" (22–23; 32). Whereas previously he had felt there was "no intermediary between life and [him]" (22; 31), something has now come between him and his own life, distancing him from himself. That something is the mental space generated by self-reflection.

Such, then, is the explanation for the blurred image his smiling face presents to him in the mirror, so that it appears to be "double" (31; 44). This is only one—albeit the most striking and psychologically revealing—of the manifestations of the theme of the double in this novel. In addition to his self-identification with "a double face, a charming Janus" (36; 52), we have also encountered, in the two previous chapters, the theme of playacting: "On my cards: 'Jean-Baptiste Clamence, play-actor'" (36; 52), Clamence informs us. Now the actor and the mask he assumes, corresponding to his chosen role, also symbolize the theme of the double. The space between the face and the mask separates the person the actor is for himself from the person he is for the audience, just like that separating the mask we put on in everyday life when we consciously attempt to create a particular impression on our fellows from the person we know ourselves to be. It is an equivalent in real, material space of the internal, mental space opened up by introspection within our own consciousness. Does Clamence not tell us that he lives his life "under a double code," so that his "most serious acts were also the ones in which [he] was the least involved" (65; 94)?

Far less obvious is the symbolic significance of two particular situations in which Clamence finds himself. The first is the incident in which he is taken to task by a bystander who accuses him of seeking to take advantage of a motorcyclist who, for his part, is at a disadvantage because he is astride his motorbike: "Taken by surprise, addressed from both sides, I had mixed everything up and the motor horns had put the finishing touch to my embarrassment" (41; 58). Caught in the middle, just as he may well feel torn between two contradictory voices resulting from his introspection, he experiences inner turmoil and confusion. The second episode finds Clamence in bed during a night of debauchery, "at a certain degree of lucid intoxication, lying . . . between two prostitutes and drained of all desire" (75; 108). This situation is similar to one in which the void of a certain introspective lucidity is marked out between two polarities corresponding, once again, to two inner voices. It should be stressed here, with regard to the interpretation of these two passages, that it is Clamence himself, as narrator, who is responsible for the precise choice of words in the evocation of the two episodes in question: it is he who has chosen to recount them in this way. Consequently, it is by no means farfetched to attribute to these two passages the symbolic meaning proposed;

inevitably, the manner in which he recalls the events to mind cannot help but be, potentially at least, psychologically revealing.

The crucial point here is that the doubling-up of himself that Clamence experiences, bringing about an impression of loss of harmony in his relationship with himself, so that he no longer feels comfortable with himself, is the inevitable product of any form of introspection, for as the consciousness reflects upon itself, it inevitably experiences a fundamental lack of coincidence with itself. To move from an awareness of this process to the conclusion that one is lacking in sincerity is but a short step, easily taken—but it is an erroneous conclusion. It is precisely this mistake that Clamence makes, and his conclusions could not be more sweeping. He says, "After prolonged research on myself, I brought out the basic duplicity of the human being" (62; 90). He mistakes an ontological condition—that is, a state of consciousness brought about by self-reflection—for a moral condition, that of deceiving oneself with regard to one's true motivation. In other words, he takes the split consciousness (what the French conveniently refer to as *dédoublement*) for moral duplicity and insincerity. Thus, in the final analysis and in spite of what was said in chapter 4 about the parodic dimension of this novel, *The Fall* remains a profoundly existentialist work in its own right. Just as Simone de Beauvoir's novel *L'Invitée* (*She Came to Stay*) embodies the scandal of the existence of the other's consciousness, Camus here depicts the scandal of self-consciousness, the dilemma brought about by excessive self-awareness.

Thus, Clamence is, in a word, far too hard on himself in his self-condemnation, setting out systematically to blacken his own self-image. He actually speaks of getting "up the case against [himself] most thoroughly" (64; 91), and the consequences could not be more devastating. It is one thing to come to the realization that one's motives are not nearly as clear-cut as one had thought them to be, and that one is unable to sort them out with any certainty, but it is quite another thing to judge oneself guilty of systematic self-deception and hence duplicity. To discover that one is not as "simple" (62; 89) and straightforward as one had thought is not the same as discovering that one is therefore duplicitous. There exists a broad spectrum between the extremes of simplicity and duplicity, the existence of which Clamence is unwilling to recognize.

The problem is that Clamence acts on, and in light of, what he believes he has discovered about himself, drawing a rigorously logical conclusion: "Since I was a liar, I would reveal this and hurl my duplicity in the face of all those imbeciles, even before they discovered it" (67; 96). He seeks a headstart on all his potential critics. He sets about deliberately disorienting his colleagues and his acquaintances in order "to destroy that flattering reputation, the thought of which threw [him] into a rage," and to this end, he seeks "to cover everything, judgement and esteem, with a cloak of ridicule": "In order to reveal to all eyes what he was made of, I wanted to break open the handsome wax figure I presented everywhere" (69; 99). To no avail. He next thinks he feels "the need to love" (73; 105) and so contracts "simultaneous loves as, at an earlier period, [he] had multiple liaisons" (74; 107). But this creates in him a veritable "loathing for love," and so he decides "to give up women, in a certain way, and to live in a state of chastity" (75; 107). Finally, "despairing of love and chastity," he tells us, "I at last told myself that there was nothing left but debauchery, a substitute for love, which quiets the laughter, restores silence and, above all, confers immortality" (75; 108). This produces the required result by enabling him to live "in a sort of fog in which the laughter became so muffled that eventually [he] ceased to notice it" (78; 112–13), until the day he found himself on the ocean liner contemplating the black speck on the ocean's surface. He eventually hits on the ideal solution, the role of judge-penitent, which enables him to accept "duplicity instead of being upset about it" (103; 149). In fact, it enables him positively to espouse duplicity as his very raison d'être.

Clamence also chooses not only to accept but to adopt wholeheartedly the idea of his own guilt. Here the problem lies in his possessing what could be called a distinct penchant for the all-or-nothing. As he says, "The idea that comes most naturally to man, as if from his very nature, is the idea of his innocence" (60; 86). The anecdote Clamence relates in support of his contention is a telling one: "We are all like that little Frenchman at Buchenwald who insisted on registering a complaint with the clerk, himself a prisoner, who was recording his arrival. A complaint? The clerk and his comrades laughed: 'Useless, old man. You don't lodge complaints here.' 'But you see, sir,' said the little Frenchman, 'my case is exceptional. I am innocent'" (60; 86). And Clamence adds, "We are all exceptional cases." As it has become clear that there is no way that he can consider himself wholly innocent, he takes it upon himself to assume a condition of complete, unmitigated guilt. Neither half-measures nor nuances are acceptable to him. Thus, he claims that "we cannot assert the innocence of anyone, whereas we can state with certainty the guilt of all" (81; 116–17). Clamence's philosophy of the all-or-nothing, while implicit rather than explicit, underlies the way he responds to his discovery that he can no longer consider himself innocent.

This same philosophy manifests itself in both the political and religious dimensions of his narrative, where it translates into totalitarianism, which is at the core of the political beliefs Clamence expresses, and of the religious absolute, the concept of a supreme deity. An examination of the political and religious dimensions of the novel will, of course, serve to flesh out the tableau of contemporary society already sketched out in the previous chapter. But these dimensions of the work also, of necessity, play an important role in any portrait of Clamence's character, for political philosophy and religious beliefs naturally constitute an essential part of a person's psychological makeup.

Clamence makes no secret of his totalitarian leanings; on the contrary, he asserts, "In philosophy as in politics, I am for any theory that refuses to grant man innocence and for any practice that treats him as guilty. You see in me, an enlightened advocate of slavery" (97; 140). "Slavery, preferably smiling," is, in his view, "inevitable" (36; 51). Not for him the hypocrisy that society likes to cultivate in such matters, for as he points out, "no man is a hypocrite in his pleasures" (49; 71). "We must not admit [the inevitability of slavery]. Isn't it better that whoever cannot do without having slaves should call them free men? As a matter of principle to begin with, and, secondly, not to drive them to despair. We owe them that compensation, don't we? In that way, they will continue to smile and we shall maintain our good conscience" (36; 51–52). The political message he conveys could not be more authoritarian. He considers that "power . . . settles everything" (35; 50) and that recourse to force is but a sign of intelligence: "The truth is that every intelligent man, as you know, dreams of being a gangster and of ruling over society by force alone. As it is not so easy as the detective novels might lead one to believe, one generally relies on politics and rushes to join the cruellest party" (42; 60–61). He clearly approves of the marked tendency in modern society to replace all dialogue with a perfunctory communiqué or decree to be obeyed without question, and indeed, this selfsame objective has been achieved and incarnated in the very form of this literary work, in which the ostensible dialogue has been reduced to what is, in effect and formally speaking, a monologue. "For the dialogue we have substituted the communiqué. 'This is the truth,' we say. 'You can discuss it as much as you want; we aren't interested. But in a few years there'll be the police to show you I'm right'" (35; 50).

Clamence's political opinions are a reflection of one of his most striking traits, his cynicism, which appears to know no bounds, as witnessed by his commentary on the Jewish district of Amsterdam: "I live in the Jewish quarter or what was called so until our Hitlerian brethren spaced it out a bit. What a clean-up! Seventy-five thousand Jews deported or assassinated; that's real vacuum-cleaning. I admire that diligence, that methodical patience!" (10; 15). It is obvious that as outrageous a statement as this one—even allowing for its black humor—poses problems for the reader, and even more so for the reader familiar with the author's previous works.

Clamence's penchant for totalitarianism transforms itself into a veritable hymn in its favor, constituting a kind of apocalyptic tableau of the modern age, with its two great rivals, fascism and communism. Its precursor was the *Ode to the Police* and *Apotheosis of the Guillotine* that Clamence had begun to write (68; 98). This chilling and haunting vision represents the powerful climax of the novel's depiction of contemporary society: "The essential is that everything should become simple, as for the child, that every act should be ordered, that good and evil should be arbitrarily. . . . pointed out. The essential is to cease being free and to obey, in repentance, a greater rogue than oneself. . . . Not to mention the fact, *cher ami*, that we must take revenge for having to die alone. Death is solitary, whereas slavery is collective. The others get theirs too, and at the same time as we—that's what counts. All together at last, but on our knees and heads bowed" (99–100; 144).

Clamence's vision is the logical and inexorable outcome of his refusal to accept and forgive himself for the foibles that he had thought to discern at the core of his existence prior to the young woman's throwing herself into the river Seine: "No excuses ever, for anyone; that's my principle at the outset" (96; 139–40). It is a logic that is terrifying in its rigor and the implacable manner in which the most natural and common human weaknesses lead to the unbridled and institutionalized reign of "power and the whip" (99; 144). Not the least terrifying aspect of this nightmarish vision is that contrary to Clamence's observation that he is "well aware that slavery is not immediately realizable" and "will be one of the blessings of the future" (100; 145), it does not properly belong to the realm of prophecy but looms large in our immediate past and present, as any survivor of the Holocaust can attest. Camus has painted a likeness of the world we live in, even if we do not care to recognize it, for its recognition implies nothing less than the end of civilization.

At the same time, this hymn to the collective slavery of the concentration camp gives full play to what is manifestly one of the most basic characteristics of Clamence's psychological makeup, his sadomasochism. One of the two components of his sadomasochism, sadism, was already present in his dealings with women, as in the episode of the woman who related his sexual deficiencies to a third party: "From that moment onwards, . . . I began . . . to mortify her in every way. I would give her up and take her back, force her to give herself at inappropriate times and in inappropriate places, treat her so brutally, in every respect, that eventually I attached myself to her as I imagine the jailor is bound to his prisoner" (48; 69–70). The absolute political power he dreams of being subjugated to, in common with all his fellows, was already foreshadowed by the absolute psychological power he craved in his past life: "I could live happily only on condition that all the individuals on earth, or the greatest possible number, were turned towards me, eternally unattached, deprived of any separate existence, and ready to answer my call at any moment, doomed in short to sterility until the day I should deign to favour them" (51; 73).

The hymn to collective servitude enables us to effect the transition to the religious dimension of *The Fall*, as was suggested by the ideal of arbitrary "good and evil." On this point, a key passage is the following: "So hurrah for the master, whoever he may be, to take the place of heaven's law. 'Our Father who art provisionally here . . . Our guides, our delightfully severe masters, O cruel and beloved leaders . . .'" (100; 144). In this passage—which finds its literary consummation in the author's short story "Le Renégat ("The Renegade")—we see that the image of omnipotence is central to both Clamence's political beliefs and his religious creed, just as violence is, for both "empires and churches are born under the sun of death" (93; 135). It is the institutionalization of arbitrary power that matters, and that alone.

The portrait of religion is motivated by the same psychological needs as the depiction of the political landscape and is, of course, no more positive or encouraging than anything else in this novel. Clamence is "inclined to see religion [as an institution], rather as a huge laundering venture" whereby "God's usefulness would be to guarantee innocence" (82; 118). As for the pope, Clamence's "great idea," as he calls it, "is that one must forgive the Pope": "To begin with, he needs it more than anyone else. Secondly, that's the only way to set oneself above him . . ." (93–94; 135). In his view, "religions are on the wrong tack the moment they start to moralize and fulminate commandments," for "God is not needed to create guilt or to punish": "Our fellow-men suffice, aided by ourselves" (81; 117). Indeed, his whole narrative is a thoroughly convincing illustration that humanity's guilt is of its own making.

Curiously, at the heart of the religious dimension of the novel is the person of Jesus, who, as a historical figure, it should be stressed, held for Camus, as much as for his character, a considerable fascination. Clamence's attitude to Christ is summed up in these words, strangely moving in the mouth of Camus's strange and perturbing fictional character: "He cried aloud his agony and that's why I love him, my friend who died without knowing" (84; 121). One senses that Camus is perhaps closest to his fictional creature in these lines: "He [Christ] simply wanted to be loved, nothing more. Of course, there are those who love him, even among Christians. But they are not numerous" (85; 122)—a critique of the avowed followers of Christianity rather than of Christianity itself or, if one prefers, of the church as a collective community rather than as a set of beliefs.[3] Here, too, Clamence has another "great idea" he is all too ready to share with us—that Christ is no more wholly innocent than each and every one of us and that he was, moreover, painfully aware of the fact: "Say, do you know why he was crucified—the one you are perhaps thinking of at this moment? . . . The real reason is that *he* knew he was not altogether innocent. If he did not bear the weight of the crime he was accused of, he had committed others—even though he didn't know which ones. Did he really not know them? He was at the source, after all; he must have heard of a certain slaughter of the innocents" (82–83; 118–19).

Before leaving the religious dimension of *The Fall*, mention must be made of its extensive and pervasive religious imagery.[4] Earlier, reference was made to the "bitter water of [his] baptism" (80; 115) and to the obvious religious connotation of the novel's title. If the waters of the river Seine are instrumental in the protagonist's baptism, the person who is thus reborn is more in the likeness of Lucifer than in that of God. Clamence's first name is, itself, significant in this respect: Jean-Baptiste (i.e., John the Baptist), with his "career as a false prophet crying in the wilderness" (107; 155). It is Clamence's plaintive and not unmoving cry "Yes, we have lost track of the light, the mornings, the holy innocence of those who forgive themselves" (106; 153) that curiously calls forth from Camus's pen the beautiful evocation of the doves, the symbols of peace, whose image is suggested by the snowflakes that cover the streets and canals of Amsterdam with a pristine purity: "Amsterdam asleep in the white night . . . —it will be purity, even if fleeting, before tomorrow's mud. See the huge flakes drifting against the window-panes. It must be the doves, surely. They finally make up their minds to come down, the little dears; they are covering the waters and the roofs with a thick layer of feathers; they are fluttering at every window. What an invasion! Let's hope they are bringing good news. Everyone will be saved, eh?—and not only the elect" (106; 153–54). Here the doves clearly symbolize Clamence's lost innocence, a last impediment to the reign of absolute guilt and a reminder of what is no more and never can be again.

Also contributing to the religious dimension of the work is the missing painting that originally formed part of Van Eyck's altarpiece, *The Adoration of the Lamb.* As far as the content of the whole altarpiece is concerned, it depicts the Christian answer to the problem of guilt, as is pointed out by Jeffrey Meyers. Like Clamence in the novel, John the Baptist, who is depicted in two of the panels, wears camel's hair. In one of the two depictions, on the vaulted arches behind his head, one reads words taken from the sermon of Petrus Chrysolus, a bishop of Ravenna, on the beheading of the saint: "This is St. John the Baptist, greater than man, equal to the angels, the sum of the law, the sanction of the Gospels, the voice of the Apostles, the silence of the Prophets, the lamp of the world, the witness of the Lord." The extravagant terms in which John the Baptist is described in this inscription appear to mirror "the misplaced egomania of Jean-Baptiste Clamence" (Meyers, 46). As for the missing panel itself, it plays a key role in advancing the actual plot as well as the symbolic meaning of the novel. Philip Rhein (156) sums up its role in these words: "From the third paragraph of the book in which Jean-Baptiste refers to an 'empty rectangle marking the place where a picture has been taken down' [6; 9] to the second last paragraph in which he reveals that in his mind the painting has become the instrument that will lead to his arrest, his subsequent beheading and the close of his career 'as a false prophet . . .' [107; 155], the altarpiece is ever-present in the reader's mind as an internal image of the novel's meaning." For this critic, it provides "a symbolic and aesthetic focus underlying the many layers of meaning contained in *The Fall*" and hence contributes to the formal unity of the work.

Having studied the political and religious themes that play so large a part in the body of Clamence's narrative and having seen how their character is a direct outcome of his psychological evolution in light of the three crucial incidents evoked earlier, we now have to bring into the picture of his psychological makeup one of the most characteristic stylistic features of this text: the prevalence of those succinct and pithy statements called "maxims." In fact, a large part of his narrative is made up of maxims and anecdotes.

Maxims are of the nature of general "truths." They consist of a broad statement concerning human nature or society that claims to enjoy universal validity. Because of their generality, they cannot characterize any single person. For this reason, in a novel narrated in the third person, they never constitute a vehicle for the characterization of fictional beings, but in the case of a first-person narrative such as *The Fall*, there is no single element of the text that does not serve to characterize the narrator, since every word of the text originates with him. Consequently, the innumerable maxims that punctuate this novel do provide illuminating information about Clamence's character. It is not, in the first instance at least, their content that tells us anything about his character but rather the choice of the maxims in question and the view of human nature and society they imply. They also fulfill a very significant role in creating complicity between Clamence the storyteller and the reader.

Many of the maxims embody what could be termed "psychological truisms," as when Clamence points out that "what we call fundamental truths are simply the ones we discover after all the others" (62; 89–90) or that "a liking for truth at any cost is a passion that spares nothing and that nothing resists. It's a vice, at times a comfort, or a selfishness" (61; 88). They encompass all aspects of human life. Many concern relationships: "True love is exceptional. Two or three times a century, more or less. The rest of the time there is vanity or boredom" (43–44; 63); and "Physical jealousy is a result of the imagination at the same time as being a self-judgement. One attributes to the rival the nasty thoughts one has oneself in the same circumstances" (78; 112). Others concern political life: "Thus the censor shouts aloud what he proscribes" (84; 120). And others, religion: "Don't wait for the Last Judgement. It takes place every day" (82; 118). The best are worthy of the great seventeenth-century French moralist La Rochefoucauld, whose work Camus greatly admired: "When one has no character one *has* to apply a method" (10; 15); and "That's the way man is, *cher* Monsieur. He has two faces: he can't love without self-love" (26–27; 38).

The countless maxims are not the least satisfying aspect of this text for its reader, but it is easy to lose sight of the fact that they, too, play their part in delineating Clamence's character. What they invariably have in common is their pessimistic message concerning human nature and psychology, which contributes to the impression of a deep-rooted and unmitigated cynicism on the part of their formulator. The person formulating them, however, is not Clamence the protagonist of the story of his past life but Clamence the storyteller. This is clear from the following: "None the less, style, like sheer silk, too often hides eczema" (7; 10). This refers to the very language he is using, as well as to that he had acquired as a lawyer to plead his clients' cases. One should also note that there is a definite psychological continuity between Clamence's state of mind subsequent to his fall from grace and his state of mind as he recounts his past life in the Amsterdam bar. (This does not, however, rule out the possibility of a subtle, but potentially highly significant shift in his frame of mind once he actually begins to act out his chosen role of judge-penitent, synonymous with his role as storyteller.) For this reason, the maxims form a bridge between the protagonist and the narrator. They also play a major role in fleshing out the psychological and, to a lesser extent, the sociological dimension of the novel and in giving to whatever message the text conveys a universal resonance.

7

Clamence the Storyteller:
The Judge-Penitent

In this chapter, I shall turn from the character and life of the Parisian lawyer to the person in the bar Mexico City whom we encounter as we begin reading *The Fall*: the judge-penitent Clamence has chosen to become. The first thing that strikes us about him is his politeness and his discretion. He seems not to want to intrude, seeking to keep his distance for fear of appearing to force himself on the person he has just met. At the same time, for some unknown reason, he gives the impression of being rather distrustful, for he says of the rather primitive, gorilla-like barkeeper, "I confess I am drawn by such creatures who are all of a piece," and then adds, "Anyone who has meditated a great deal on man . . . is led to feel nostalgia for the primates. They at least don't have any ulterior motives" (6; 8). This suggests that he harbors some suspicion of other people's motives.

He is more than willing to talk, however, once he has struck up a conversation. He speaks of his "communicative nature" (6; 9), and indeed, he needs little encouragement to pursue his remarks about both himself and the immediate surroundings. We can well believe him when he says, "I am talkative, alas, and make friends easily. Although I know how to keep my distance, I seize . . . every opportunity

(6; 9). The note of regret expressed by the exclamation "alas"—unless it reflects a certain self-indulgence—could suggest that he feels his talkativeness makes him in some way vulnerable. This appears to be confirmed later when he says, "When I see a new face, something inside me sounds the alarm. 'Slow! Danger!' Even when the attraction is strongest, I am on my guard" (10; 15). Be that as it may, his loquaciousness is matched only by his eloquence, and he explicitly confesses his "weakness . . . for fine speech" (7; 10).

His sense of humor is very much in evidence, as when he mentions the "four million silhouettes" who inhabit Paris, adding, "Nearly five million at the last census? Why, they must have multiplied. And that wouldn't surprise me. It always seemed to me that our fellow-citizens had two passions: ideas and fornication" (7; 10). It is true that the would-be humorous comments of this compulsive talker—who rightly says of himself, "As soon as I open my mouth, sentences pour out" (11; 16–17)—can at times be grating, as was the case with his comments on the former Jewish quarter of Amsterdam quoted earlier (10; 15). In fact, humor often gives way to unmitigated sarcasm, at the expense of hypocrisy, as when he says, "Slavery?—certainly not, we are against it! That we should be forced to have it in our homes or in our factories—well, that's natural; but boasting about it, that's the limit!" (34; 49). Such sarcasm nonetheless betrays the same deep-rooted cynicism mentioned earlier: "'I beg you to believe in my sympathetic understanding' in the inner discourse always precedes immediately 'and now, let's turn to other matters'" (24–25; 35).

As for his physical appearance, he describes himself in these terms: "By my stature, my shoulders, and this face that I have often been told was shy, I look rather like a football player." But he immediately qualifies this by adding, "But if I am judged by my conversation it must be allowed I have a little subtlety" (9; 13–14). He also comments on the threadbare condition of his coat, which contrasts with his manicured nails, and draws attention to the contradictory impression he is thus likely to create: "I . . . am sophisticated, and yet I confide in you without caution on the sole basis of your looks. Finally, despite my good manners and my fine speech, I frequent sailors' bars on the Zeedijk" (9; 14). He concludes by reiterating the nature of his present

THE FALL

profession, which appears to sum up the contradictions manifest in his person: "My profession is double, that's all, like the human being. . . . I am a judge-penitent" (9–10; 14).

There is something intriguing about this garrulous frequenter of the bar Mexico City. Why is he so insistent in spite of his earlier apparent reticence and his numerous declarations of not wishing to intrude? What is it that he wants exactly? Why can he not stop talking and put a halt to the unending stream of chatter? It goes without saying that the curious profession he claims for himself, that of judge-penitent, can only add to the fascination he exerts as a character. The need to clarify and better understand what exactly such a profession consists of is reason enough to want to get to know him better. It successfully counters any impatience his incessant chatter might provoke in his listener. The second chapter opens appropriately with the words "What is a judge-penitent?" (15; 21). And the rest of the novel is, in a sense, but an extended answer to that question.

It soon becomes transparently clear that the speaker has very little faith in what we like to call human nature. Take friendship, for example. "Have you never suddenly needed understanding, help, friendship?" he asks. "Yes, of course. I have learned to be satisfied with understanding. It is found more readily" (24; 35). Friendship is not, in his view, all that it is made out to be, for "it is long and hard to obtain but when one has it there's no getting rid of it; one simply has to cope with it" (25; 35). To enjoy friendship, it is necessary to incur obligations that will always weigh on you. Moreover, contrary to what might be assumed, the obligations incurred do not turn out to be reciprocal ones; friends are *never* there when they are needed: "Don't think for a minute that your friends will telephone you every evening, as they ought to, in order to find out if this doesn't happen to be the evening when you are deciding to commit suicide, or simply whether you don't need company, whether you are not in the mood to go out. No, don't worry, they'll ring up the evening you are not alone, when life is beautiful" (25; 35–36). Similarly, he warns us to beware whenever our friends ask us to be sincere with them, for "they merely hope you will encourage them in the good opinion they have of themselves by providing them with the additional assurance they find in your promise of

64

sincerity." His advice could not be more cynical: "Promise to tell the truth and lie as best you can. You will satisfy their hidden desire and doubly prove your affection" (61; 88).

Clamence's attitude to friendship, based, it is reasonable to assume, on past experience, is summed up by his exclamation "May heaven protect us, *cher* Monsieur, from being set on a pedestal by our friends!" (25; 36). It is easy to deduce from this disillusioned commentary on friendship—which, rather than pointing out its limitations, insists on its deceptiveness and its utter inadequacy in fulfilling our expectations—that Clamence's existence has been singularly lacking in real friendship of any kind.

The catalytic role of death in relation to our feelings provides a further sad commentary on human nature as Clamence conceives it: "Have you noticed that death alone awakens our feelings?" (26; 37). We never love any living person as much as we love those who are no longer with us: "How we love the friends who have just left us? How we admire those of our teachers who have ceased to speak, their mouths filled with earth?"—the reason being that "with them there is no obligation" (26; 37). In short, the speaker has clearly lost any faith he may have had in human nature: "That's the way man is, *cher* Monsieur. He has two faces: he can't love without self-love" (26–27; 38).

Needless to say, Clamence does not exclude himself from this generalization. The sign that would most appropriately represent him, he tells us, is "a double face, a charming Janus" (36; 52), even if he later makes this further highly enigmatic comment on his physiognomy: "Alas, after a certain age every man is responsible for his face. Mine . . . But what matter?" (43; 62). His facial features are thus left to the imagination; all the reader is told is how meaningful those features are. It is for him or her to decide what those features are, and only then can he or she set out to determine what their meaning might be.

On the theme of friendship and love, Clamence is no less forthcoming in his remarks. As was noted earlier, "true love" he considers "exceptional": "Two or three times a century, more or less" (43; 63). As for what he calls "the love promised by books," he has "never encountered [it] in life" (74; 106–7), although it is not that he has not looked for it, for he has, as he tells us, "felt the need to love" (73;

105). And so Clamence has known neither love nor friendship. Paradoxically—for an unbeliever—the only friendship he will admit to is that which he feels "for the first Christian of all" (99; 144), Christ.

Underlying the themes of love and friendship, because of their depiction in wholly negative terms, is their opposite: solitude, although solitude is rarely discussed explicitly. The very insistence with which he comes back, time and again, to the subject of friendship is significant in itself, and the striking and all-pervasive cynicism with which love and friendship are referred to only serves to disguise the importance they clearly have for the speaker. These considerations impart a particular resonance to his remark that "for anyone who is alone, without God and without a master, the weight of days is dreadful" (98; 141). For if freedom is a source of anguish, man's essential solitude is no less so.

It is, in fact, easy for the reader to overlook the fundamental solitude to which this insistent monologue gives such poignant expression. The endless, apparently inexhaustible stream of words is, among other things, a cry for help and a reaching out toward the other person— whoever he may be. Does he not at one point appeal to his companion to "drink up" with him, adding by way of an explanation: "I need your understanding"? "I see this declaration amazes you," he comments. "Have you never suddenly needed understanding, help, friendship?" (24; 35). And then he leaves it at that. The point has been made, nonetheless, and it is left to the reader to draw the appropriate conclusions.

This aspect of the novel confers on the character of the judge-penitent a tragic dimension, which must not be underestimated if we are to appreciate fully the impact this text has on its reader. There are only occasional intimations of the anguish that he clearly does his best to conceal for reasons which will later become apparent, such as his remark that "I don't know how to name the odd feeling that comes over me. Isn't it shame perhaps? . . . that emotion has never left me since the adventure I found at the heart of my memory" (51; 74). These occasional fleeting glimpses of his true feelings confirm his statement, right at the end of the novel, that his "solution is not the ideal" (106; 152–53), in spite of the brave face he seeks to put on: "The eyes of the soul—to be sure—if there is a soul and it has eyes! But you see, we're not sure, we can't be sure. Otherwise, there would be a solution; at least one could get oneself taken seriously" (55*; 79).[1] Clamence is, in spite of himself, a truly tragic and poignant figure who, like all such fictional characters, has indeed fallen from a great height—even if, in his case, the height in question is merely that of his own high opinion of himself. There is good reason to believe that the need to break out of this devastating inner solitude provides the essential motivation for the "solution" that he has hit upon, the profession of judge-penitent, for "death is solitary, whereas slavery is collective" (100; 144). That is why "without slavery, . . . there is," in his eyes, "no definitive solution" (97; 140).

We find the confirmation of this particular function of his role of judge-penitent in the following remarks: "I've lost that lucidity to which my friends used to enjoy paying respects. I say 'my friends,' moreover, as a matter of principle. I have no more friends; I have nothing but accomplices. To make up for this, their number has increased; they are the whole human race" (55, 78–79). Since nobody can be pronounced innocent, not even the pope or Christ himself, we have the consolation that there does exist something which binds us all together, all without exception, and that is our shared guilt. Within this generalized guilt we all have our place, we all belong, once and for all. Nobody is excluded. This universal guilt can, Clamence feels, serve to bring the whole human race together in a common condition. For want of friends, accomplices will fill the bill, for both friends and accomplices have something in common: the fact of sharing, whether the thing shared be an activity of some kind or friendship itself. The communality of Clamence's solution can easily be lost sight of when he points out that he "had to find another means of extending judgement to everybody in order to make it weigh less heavily on [his] own shoulders" (100; 145), adding that this was because "one had to overwhelm oneself to have the right to judge others" (101; 146). There is no doubt of the truth of this explanation. But the fact remains that such a strategy at one and the same time has the effect of alleviating his sense of solitude. The function of judge-penitent then is, in a sense, his own response to the cry from the heart, a cry for help that can, if we are sufficiently attentive, be heard echoing throughout Clamence's monologue: "Everyone will be saved, eh!—and not only the elect" (106; 154). That this is not, of course, its only function we shall see in a moment.

First of all, however, let us consider another possible function not of the role of judge-penitent as such but of Clamence's loquaciousness, referred to earlier. There is another psychological need that his incessant chatter—so compulsive that his companion can hardly get a word in—can be seen to fulfill, one arising from the crucial incident on the bridge over the Seine. The young woman's fall was directly responsible, as we have seen, for Clamence's own fall. Now, the unending stream of words that pour out of his mouth, offering his listener not a moment's respite, could well represent an effort on his part to put an end to his impression of falling. It could well be his way of attempting to regain control over the psychological situation he finds himself in: a state of free-fall, giddying and wholly disorienting in its effect on him, undermining his entire being, mind and body. The language he is unceasingly generating has the effect of giving him something to cling to in the general confusion, something outside of himself and yet originating from within himself, the autonomous existence of which constitutes a point of stability to counter and potentially arrest the impression of falling. This could be reason enough for his volubleness.

There is, in fact, a good deal of imagery in *The Fall* that evokes the impression of falling.[2] It should be pointed out straight away that it is precisely on the level of the imagery that translations of any literary work reveal their inadequacy, for a given word in French does not, by any means, always translate into the same word in the English text, the meaning of words being always determined by their context. A good example of this is when Clamence says that it is too difficult for him to *se maintenir* (120)—that is, to keep himself in the same position and hence prevent himself from falling—and to continue. The impression suggested by the French expression for an activity that runs exactly counter to that of falling is somewhat attenuated in the English translation: "He found it too hard for him *to hold on* and continue. It was better to have done with it . . . and to go elsewhere where perhaps he would be upheld" (83; my emphasis). At all events, such a passage clearly describes someone in danger of falling.

The impression of falling is created in particular by images of sliding and slipping. For example, when Clamence is speaking of his past life in Paris, he says, "Everything slid off—yes, just slid off me" (38*; 54). Associated with sliding or slipping is the movement of skimming or barely brushing the surface of something. Thus, he speaks of moving forward merely "on the surface of life, in the realm of words as it were, never in reality": "All those books barely read, those friends barely loved, those cities barely visited, those women barely possessed!" (38–39; 55). Contact is minimal, only in passing, and so one loses hold and with it, any stability, so that everything just slips by, like one's surroundings once one begins to fall. "The question is," he says, "how to slip through and above all—yes, above all, the question is how to elude judgement" (57; 82). A similar image even characterizes the sound of his own voice as he is, borne along and hence supported by the momentum of his own discourse: "My own voice would lead me on and I would follow it; without really soaring, as I used to do, I at least got off the ground and did a little hedge-hopping" (79; 114). Note that the French expression *faire du rase-mottes* involves skimming across the ground much closer to the surface than *hedge-hopping* in English, as when one throws a pebble so that it will skim across the surface of a lake. As was suggested earlier, his compulsive talk could well represent an attempt to gain a foothold in external reality, in the world outside his own mind, and thereby arrest the sensation of falling.

There are also instances where it is not a question of physically slipping but of an abstract use of the same word, as when Clamence refers to freedom: "With that keyword I would bludgeon whoever contradicted me . . . I used to whisper it in bed in the ear of my sleeping partners and it helped me to drop them. I could slip it . . ." (97*; 140). He also speaks of slipping over something quickly in the course of his conversation without pausing to comment on it and as though wishing not to draw attention to it. Having mentioned "a masculine guild too often reviled," he adds, "But I'll slip over that" (77*; 111).

But even such metaphorical uses of the same word are no less significant in the present context, for reasons I shall explain in a moment.

All these evocations of slipping and sliding suggest a movement out of control, symptomatic of the free-fall that Clamence's existence has become for him. The image that sums up his situation is, above all, the "little-ease": the dungeon cell that was "not high enough to stand up in nor yet wide enough to lie down in" and that obliged its occupant "to live on the diagonal" (81; 116), with the result that "sleep was a fall" (81*; 116).

Falling is inevitably accompanied by a sense of disorientation. We have already seen in chapter 4 the disorienting effect created by the colorless and monotonous Dutch landscape and seascape: "With its flat shores, lost in the fog, there's no knowing where it begins or ends," Clamence says of the Zuyderzee. "So we are steaming along without any landmark" (72; 103), just as in falling, we lose all our bearings, not knowing where we are anymore. And darkness does not help in finding one's bearings: "The earth is dark, *cher ami*, the coffin thick, and the shroud opaque" (55; 79). The very progression through the concentric circles of Amsterdam's canals represents a journey into darkness: "When one comes from the outside, as one gradually goes through those circles, life . . . becomes denser, darker. Here, we are in the last circle" (13; 18–19), where it must, by definition, be difficult to make out anything at all.

Disorientation can also take the form of a person's feeling disconcerted, which is the way the English translator has chosen to render the French word *désorienter* in the passages in which Clamence says that "by repeating these pleasant indiscretions, I merely succeeded in disconcerting opinion somewhat" (70; 101) and that those of his clients who are more sentimental than intelligent are "disconcerted at once" (103; 149) by his apparent confession.

It is important to stress here that it is the storyteller's narrative that creates, through its imagery, a falling effect. Even though some of the quoted passages refer to Clamence's life as a Parisian lawyer before the incident on the bridge, the precise character of the image is determined by the manner in which the judge-penitent now chooses to relate those past events rather than by their exact nature. And his narration takes place, of course, some time after the young woman's drowning and is thus contemporaneous with the state he finds himself in as a result of his own fall from grace. Some of the examples are, in fact, little more than turns of phrase or metaphorical uses of the vocabulary of falling, as we saw earlier. If they evoked any precise visual image or image of movement at all, it was only fleetingly, so that the reader would scarcely register the fact. It is only when one takes into account the totality of Clamence's narrative, including not only the images employed but also the indeterminateness of the forms and figures barely emerging from the watery and foggy Amsterdam atmosphere, the copper-colored tint of the description of the Dutch Lohengrin "dreamily riding their black bicycles . . . in circles" and "sleepwalking in the fog's gilded incense" (12; 18), with its autumnal connotations, and the slippery nature of Clamence's discourse itself as the reader experiences it, that it is possible to appreciate fully how the imagery of this novel is a direct reflection of its title. That his narrative should also illustrate the narrator's fundamental predicament is, of course, hardly surprising.

Countering the image of falling is that of soaring or gliding, representing complementary movements, the first upward and the second downward. It is significant that this image characterizes his life before the fall. Then, his voice used to "soar" (9; 114). In fact, as he puts it, "I soared until the evening when . . ." (24; 34). This soaring movement is, of course, not unrelated to his love of heights, and heights have still not lost their attraction for him in spite of all his newfound awareness of their psychological implications: "After all, living aloft is still the only way of being seen and hailed by the greatest number" (21; 30). Before the detailed description of Clamence's solution at the end of the novel, there are a number of images of ascension that give a hint of what is to come. Clamence remarks, for instance, that "too many people now climb on the cross merely to be seen from a greater distance" (84; 121), and he asks himself, "Should I climb up to the pulpit, like many of my illustrious contemporaries, and curse humanity?" (101; 145–46).

What comes is Clamence's veritable apotheosis whereby once and for all—or so he believes—he will have put an end to that sinking feeling that had been undermining his every waking moment and reenacting time and again his fall from grace: "Since finding my solution, I yield to everything, to women, to pride, to boredom, to resentment, and even to the fever that I feel delightfully *rising* at this moment. I dominate at last. . . . Once more I have found a height to which I am the only one to climb and from which I can judge everybody" (104; 150; my emphasis). It is the feeling of rising up and reaching a great height: "I grow taller, *très cher*, I grow taller, I breathe freely, I am on the mountain, the plain stretches before my eyes" (104; 151). Any impression of falling is now banished for good: "I sit enthroned among my bad angels *at the summit* of the Dutch heaven and I watch *ascending* towards me, as they issue from the fogs and the water, the multitude of the Last Judgement. They *rise* slowly . . ." (105; 151; my emphasis). The sense of height is not only imaginary but also characterizes his situation in relation to his companion listening to him: "Yes, I am moving about. How could I remain in bed like a good patient? I must be higher than you, and my thoughts lift me up" (105; 151–52). The apotheosis reaches its climax with the image of his overshadowing the earth like an evil angel: "Soaring over this whole continent which is under my sway without knowing it, drinking in the absinthe-coloured light of breaking day [with its association with the rising sun], intoxicated with bad words, I am happy—I am happy, I tell you, I won't let you think I am not happy, I am happy unto death!" (105; 152). It is true that Clamence's insistence on his newfound happiness does not ring altogether true. It is as though he is trying to convince himself, as much as his listener, of his happiness. Here, we glimpse once again that tragic dimension that he retains to the very end and that makes of him a character capable not only of intriguing us, but also of moving us.

And so, Clamence finally manages to regain the heights for which he has so great a predilection and from which he had been toppled by his gradual discovery of those home truths examined in the previous chapter. Now he has found the way to gain permanent ascendency over all, to enjoy a buoyant superiority that places him out of reach, thereby rendering him invulnerable. Yet, at the same time, while arresting once and for all his fateful fall and redressing the situation, the profession of judge-penitent does not leave him high and dry like

God the Father (even if, as he says, he feels like him [104; 151]). On the contrary, it serves to alleviate his sense of inner solitude by creating a genuine community, albeit a community of shared guilt, to which he can be sure of belonging and in which he can take up his rightful place. This community comprises nothing less than the whole of the human race, including not only the pope but also the historical figure of Jesus Christ. In the final analysis and within a literary and intellectual (not to mention autobiographical) context, the community he thus brings into being acquires a distinctly parodic resonance: it takes on all the appearance of a parody of that human condition the existentialist writers set out to depict.

Having now seen how Clamence's highly inventive solution to his dilemma can be understood as a response to his most fundamental psychological needs brought about by the personal crisis of his fall, it finally remains for us to examine in detail the precise nature of his role of judge-penitent.

Once he has brought to light what he considers to be the true motivation underlying the whole of his past life and asserted the impossibility of his innocence and hence the certainty of his guilt, he feels "vulnerable and as if [he] were handed over to public accusation": "The circle of which I was the centre broke and [my fellows] lined up in a row as on the judges' bench" (58; 83). In order to break out of his solitary situation, which any accused person finds himself in, "it is essential to begin by extending the condemnation to all, without distinction, in order to thin it out at the start" (96; 103), for "it is not enough to accuse yourself in order to clear yourself. One must accuse oneself in a certain way," which it will take "a considerable time to perfect" (70; 101). He realizes that "inasmuch as one couldn't condemn others without immediately judging oneself, one had to overwhelm oneself to have the right to judge others" (101; 146). In order not to find oneself alone in the prisoner's dock, one has to be in a position to condemn one's fellows, and yet, in order to be able to do so—that is, have the right to do so—one must first of all condemn oneself. Put in these terms, Clamence's dilemma appears insoluble. The ingenious solution he hits upon is to "overwhelm" himself with unmitigated guilt so as to encourage his fellows to

assume no less a degree of guilt out of sympathy for, and empathy
with, his predicament. Thereby, he finds a "means of extending judgement to everybody in order to make it weigh less heavily on [his] own
shoulders" (100; 145).

The final masterly stroke of his solution is the key to the success
of the whole enterprise: to turn an apparent confession into an
inescapable accusation, to slip out of the prisoner's dock at the very
moment that the other person, his listener, voluntarily enters it. This
constitutes the coup de grâce. He sets about building up "a portrait
which is the image of all and of no one," and then "I show it with
great sorrow: 'This, alas, is what I am!' The prosecutor's charge is finished. But at the same time the portrait I hold out to my contemporaries becomes a mirror" (102; 148).

Just how he manages to slip out of the prisoner's dock at the very
last moment will be discussed in the next chapter, since the details of
the strategy he adopts to achieve this end concern the evolution of his
relationship with the companion he is speaking to, and it is to this
character that I shall turn next.

8

Clamence's Unseen Companion

Not the least remarkable aspect of this work is its form. In the world of the Amsterdam bar Mexico City, a conversation takes place—a conversation that Clamence strikes up with a complete stranger—and this conversation is continued in a variety of settings in and around the Dutch capital. In a sense, then, *The Fall* is perhaps most accurately described as the story of a conversation. Indeed, in the course of the next chapter, the appropriateness of describing the novel in this way, rather than as the story of the life and times of a certain Jean-Baptiste Clamence, will become clear. So far, I have explored the past life and the psychological makeup of Clamence and the identity and role of judge-penitent he has already assumed when the novel begins. Only now is it possible to broach the core of the novel and the real subject of this remarkable work of fiction.

In spite of the fact that Clamence's conversation with his companion is center stage, we are never given the opportunity to hear the other half of the conversation. The only voice we encounter, the only words we hear, are those of Clamence himself. This is one reason why we may be more aware of the tale of his past life than of his actual activity as a storyteller. It is easy to be taken up by the details of his past exploits and the dramatic events that come between him and his self-esteem. Their interest for the reader is obvious: the reader is looking to the tale of his previous life to throw light on both the exact nature of the profession of judge-penitent and the reason for his having chosen it.

Although there is no doubt that a conversation takes place which only comes to a close with the ending of the novel itself, the form of the novel is not that of a dialogue but that of a monologue. This is the paradox that lies at the heart of this work: the world of the novel is taken up by two characters conversing together, even though the reader is confronted with a monologue, albeit a dramatic monologue in the theatrical sense of that term. Since the whole text consists of Clamence's monologue, his unheard companion can only come to life for the reader through Clamence's own words. They alone can create the presence of that other person to whom Clamence speaks. I shall now examine how his presence is suggested by Clamence's discourse.

Clamence's companion is referred to in the opening words of the novel as the person being addressed: "May I, Monsieur, offer my services without running the risk of intruding? I fear you may not be able to make yourself understood by the worthy gorilla who presides over the fate of this establishment" (5; 7). He is thus represented—or, more precisely, designated—by the verbs in the second person that complement the first-person verbs designating the speaker, Clamence. He is addressed but never represented as such, so that his presence is merely implied by the form of the speaker's remarks. In fact, of the thirteen sentences going to make up the first paragraph of the novel, six contain forms of the second-person pronoun and two refer to "Monsieur."

It is not only the unseen character's presence that is indirectly suggested, but also his words. Thus, within the very first paragraph, we read, "Now, I shall withdraw, Monsieur, happy to have been of help to you. Thank you; I'd accept if I were sure of not being a nuisance" (5; 7–8). It is clear that the second sentence is formulated in response to his companion's invitation to join him at the bar or at his table, as the case may be: "You are too kind. Then I shall bring my glass over beside yours" (5; 8). So ends the first paragraph.

The next paragraph begins, "You are right. His dumbness is deafening" (5; 8), with Clamence thus repeating the other's words referring to the bar owner and thereby rendering them, for once, explicit. Clamence goes on to describe the bar owner's activities "entertaining sailors of all nationalities" before asking his companion, "With such duties wouldn't you think that there might be some fear that his ignorance would be uncomfortable?" and then appealing to his imagination by saying, "Fancy the Cro-Magnon man lodged in the Tower of Babel!" (5; 8). Clamence continues to describe the barkeep until, at the end of the following paragraph, he once again uses the second-person pronoun: "In that respect society has somewhat spoiled, you must admit, the frank simplicity of his nature" (6; 9). The following paragraph begins: "Mind you, I'm not judging him."

The first reference to a reaction on the part of the other person follows three sentences later: "If that be foolish . . . Ah, I see you smile at that use of the subjunctive" (6–7; 9–10). The same technique is used to evoke other people present in the bar with them. For example, Clamence ends an anecdote about the last wars of religion in Europe by recounting that the militia entered the home of a pacifist who had written on his door the words "Wherever you come from, come in and be welcome" and then "disembowelled him." The next paragraph immediately begins, "Oh, pardon, Madame! But she didn't understand a word of it anyway" (11; 16). There is no questioning the skill the novelist displays in this humorous aside in what is by no means an easy task as far as novelistic technique is concerned.

Subsequently, Clamence responds to the suggestion that they "have another gin" and asks his companion whether he will be staying long in Amsterdam. "A beautiful city, isn't it?" he says. "Fascinating? There's an adjective I haven't heard for some time" (7; 10). Once again, since Clamence repeats the other's remark, the reader learns exactly what he has said.

Having next talked about Paris and its inhabitants, Clamence finally introduces himself: "But allow me to introduce myself: Jean-Baptiste Clamence, at your service. Pleased to know you. You are in business, no doubt?" (8; 12). He again, conveniently for the reader, repeats the answer he receives to his question: "In a way? Excellent reply! Judicious too: in all things we are merely 'in a way'" (8–9; 12). This gives Clamence the opportunity to "play the detective," as he puts it, while at the same time giving the author the occasion to flesh out the character of his interlocutor: "You are my age in a way, with the sophisticated eye of the man in his forties who has seen everything, in a way; you are well dressed in a way, that is as people are in our country; and your hands are smooth. Hence a bourgeois, in a way! But a cultured bourgeois! Smiling at the use of the subjunctive, in fact, proves your culture twice over because you recognize it to begin with and then because you feel superior to it. Lastly, I amuse you. And be it said without vanity, this implies in you a certain open-mindedness. Consquently you are in a way . . . But no matter" (9; 12–3). We also learn that he has possessions and has not shared them with the poor, making of him, or so Clamence claims, "a Sadducee" (9; 13). And the fact that he understands Clamence's biblical reference proves that he knows the Scriptures.

However, to speak of Camus "fleshing out" his character is to go too far, for once we have learned roughly how old he is, that he is well dressed and has smooth hands and the culture associated with the French bourgeoisie, things are left at that, and the focus turns away from him as Clamence now speaks of his own person, leaving his companion in the dark as far as the reader is concerned. In fact, it is not until the very last chapter of the novel that the spotlight finally returns to the interlocutor (107; 155), when it takes the form of the inescapable, blinding light behind which sits the interrogator mercilessly questioning his victim.

In between times, the little more we discover of the character and person of Clamence's interlocutor is meager indeed. We learn that he is "courteous" (11; 16) and that he has read Dante: "Here, we are in the last circle . . . The circle of the . . . Ah, you know that? By heaven, you become harder to classify" (13; 19), remarks Clamence, adding that this proves he is "a sensitive man." In fact, later Clamence actually puts the question to him: "Do you know Dante? Really? Well I'll be damned!" (62–89). From the talk about the painting *The Just Judges*, we also learn that his culture has perhaps "some gaps" (94; 136), and the fact that he asks Clamence why he did not return the stolen painting prompts the latter to attribute to him "a policeman's reflex" (95; 137). All these details add up to very little and are certainly far from constituting a character portrait of the person in question.

The second-person pronoun serves to designate his companion without revealing who he is, and so the presence of the unseen listener has to be divined by the reader in the spaces between certain of the speaker's sentences. This, together with some of Clamence's questions that appear to echo directly his companion's own words, is all there is in the text to evoke the other character. This second character is merely there by implication. For the reader, he resembles the Dutch people in that he is "here and elsewhere" (11; 17), within the fictional world of the novel but outside the pages of the actual text.

Equally significant is the fact that, for the reader, he remains very much an unknown quantity. This is, of course, a consequence of his not being portrayed directly, for his own sake, as a character, by either an omniscient narrator in a third-person narrative or as a protagonist in a story told by a first-person narrator. If he had played a role in Clamence's past life and thereby featured in the tale told by the judge-penitent, his novelistic status would have been quite different, and there would have existed no impediment to the reader's getting to know him. Nonetheless, he remains not so much a mystery—given the fact that the reader is unaware of any particular need to learn who he is—as an unseen presence, a shadow cast over the bar or bar table at which they both sit, and little more. That the only other character in the novel is, and remains to the end, an unknown quantity will prove to be of the utmost significance when I examine the role of the reader in the next chapter.

The peculiarity of the situation in *The Fall* lies in the fact that the normal distinction between fiction and narration—that is, between story told and its telling—has become blurred. That is why I refer to Clamence as a storyteller rather than as a narrator. There is often in novels a fictional situation corresponding to the narrative level of the text constituted by the implied circumstances in which the narrator finds himself, temporally and physically, in relation to the events he is recounting. Here that narrative level of the work and the fictional situation it implies take on a life of their own and acquire all the attributes of a fictional universe in their own right. Thus, as I stated in chapter 4, Amsterdam has at least as much reality as a material presence for the reader as does the city of Paris.

Consequently, there is not the slightest doubt of the interlocutor's existence since his presence is not only frequently evoked, albeit by implication, but, as was mentioned in chapter 4, with only one exception the reader is brought back to the Dutch setting where their conversation is taking place at the beginning and end of chapters 2 to 5, in the course of which the reader may well find all his or her attention occupied by the depiction of the events of Clamence's past life. As for the remaining chapters (the first and last), they are both very largely given over to the evocation of the bar Mexico City and Clamence's bedroom, respectively.

Having established the manner in which the interlocutor's presence is conjured up for the reader, together with the fact that the person Clamence gradually gets to know during the course of their lengthy conversations remains a complete stranger to the reader, hovering as a shadowy presence not in the background but in the foreground (a crucial distinction, as will later become apparent), I will now trace the evolution of the relationship that develops between them. The nature of their interaction, in general, and the impact on the interlocutor that Clamence's discourse produces, in particular, determine the unique character of the reading experience provided by *The Fall*.

Given the passivity of his interlocutor, it is Clamence who is wholly responsible for the nature of the relationship that develops between himself and his companion. It is he who conducts and controls the course of their one-sided conversation. From the beginning, he seeks the tacit agreement of his listener to the observations he is making, although initially he does so in the most discreet manner possible, as when he says of the barkeep, "In that respect society has somewhat spoiled, *you must admit*, the frank simplicity of his nature" (6; 9; my emphasis). When his companion smiles at his use of the subjunctive, he readily concedes a weakness for fine speech and stresses that he is not lacking in critical self-awareness: "A weakness that I criticize in myself, believe me. I am well aware that an addiction to silk underwear does not necessarily imply that one's feet are dirty. None the less, style, like sheer silk, too often hides eczema" (7; 10). His companion can but approve of such a well-developed critical sense exercised at the speaker's own expense. It would be surprising, moreover, if his listener did not prove susceptible, to some degree at least, to Clamence's ready wit. Having claimed that modern man can be summed up in the single statement "He fornicated and read the papers," he adds, "After that vigorous definition, the subject will be, if I may say so, exhausted" (7; 11). Clamence plays on the expression "exhausting a subject of conversation" and the state of sexual exhaustion. Clamence's witticisms, inasmuch as his listener appreciates them, soon begin to create in his companion a sense of complicity with Clamence.

Moreover, a maxim serves as the pretext for this last quip, and as I noted earlier, his discourse is punctuated by such maxims. It is not difficult to obtain another person's concurrence with the content of a maxim, because a maxim expresses a truth of the most general kind, a truth that does not involve a very personal commitment on the part of the person acknowledging its appropriateness. To the extent that all generalizations are as true as they are false—and vice versa—it is not difficult for them to meet with an agreement that is equally general. In other words, maxims can serve as a very convenient common ground between people who, in other respects, may possess very diverse particular opinions. Thus, one cannot overestimate the significance of the role played by maxims in *The Fall*, both in drawing the interlocutor closer to Clamence by creating a sense of complicity and in singularly failing to impart to the listener any substantive information concerning the character of the speaker.

By the time Clamence's companion is subjected to approving comments about Hitler's thinning out of the Jewish population of Amsterdam, referring to it, as "real vacuum-cleaning" (10; 15), he is beginning to feel reasonably well disposed to the former Parisian lawyer. Although the black humor of these remarks is bound to introduce a potentially discordant note into their relationship and could well give Clamence's unseen companion pause, there is no indication of any protestation on his part and Clamence quickly goes on, more reassuringly, to catalog the event in more orthodox terms as "one of the greatest crimes in history." This enables his scandalous would-be witticism to be quickly thrust aside as a temporary aberration of which too much should not be made.

If his interlocutor may be beginning to feel a trifle suspicious of Clamence's alacrity in pouring out his opinions on everything that comes to hand, if not to mind, he may find some comfort in the fact that Clamence himself comments on what he calls his "natural inclination carrying [him] towards what [he] likes": "When I see a new face, something inside me sounds the alarm. 'Slow! Danger!' Even when the attraction is strongest, I am on my guard" (10; 15). Paradoxically, these remarks reassure his listener. He is now likely to feel that having chosen to impose upon himself this degree of cautiousness, Clamence, far from soliciting his listener's unquestioning acceptance of all his observations and opinions, must expect nothing less of his companion in relation to what he is listening to. Clamence does, after all, voluntarily draw attention to his excessive volubleness by referring to his "overflow" (11; 16). In spite of immediate appearances, so open an acknowledgment of characteristics with potentially dangerous consequences for his listener encourages Clamence's companion to lower his guard, rather than the contrary.

There remains, however, a need for caution. If the reason Clamence has a particular liking for the Dutch is that they are "here and elsewhere" (11; 17), then there may be some justification in suspecting that he, too, is perhaps, in a way, "here and elsewhere." If, in spite of his obtrusive presence, there is a part of him that remains inaccessible and out of reach, as private as the rest appears to be public, then appearances may prove to be deceptive. He may only appear to be open and forthcoming.

It is not, nonetheless, as though he hesitates to contradict his listener: "You are like everybody else; you take these good people for a tribe of syndics and merchants counting up their gold crowns together with their chances of eternal life. . . . *You are wrong*" (12; 177; my emphasis). He does appeal quite brazenly to his companion's vanity, calling him "a cultured bourgeois": "I amuse you. And be it said without vanity, this implies in you a certain open-mindedness" (9; 13). Here again, a paradoxical effect may be attributed to the literary skill of the author: by denying any vanity on his own part, the speaker exercises considerable subtlety in getting his companion to attribute to himself a similar lack of vanity. He thus ensures that his companion feels free to give full rein to his susceptibility (which he shares with all of us) to Clamence's shameless, self-serving flattery. Who would not be flattered, after all, to be deemed interesting by such an intriguing and fascinating person, as when Clamence remarks: "So you know the Scriptures? Decidedly, you interest me" (9; 13)?

His listener cannot fail to be impressed and reassured by Clamence's insistence on drawing attention to his own shortcomings. After his lyrical, indeed poetic, commentary on the Dutch Lohengrins cycling dreamily through the Amsterdam "fog's guilded incense," Clamence interjects, "But I am letting myself go! I am pleading a case! Forgive me." Moreover, the motivation he ascribes to himself seems innocent enough and not the least suspect: "Habit, Monsieur, vocation, also the desire to make you fully understand this city, and the heart of things!" (12–13; 18). If his aim may seem ambitious and filled with philosophical portent, it nevertheless appears to be perfectly well intentioned.

By the end of the first chapter, there is good reason to believe that Clamence has managed to build up a certain rapport with his listener and that the latter has developed a definite interest in what Clamence has to say, not to mention an undoubted curiosity about his profession of judge-penitent. It is, however, significant that the chapter draws to a close with Clamence assuming the role of tempter: "Those persons perfume themselves with spices. You go in, they draw the curtains and the navigation begins. The gods come down on to the naked bodies and the islands are set adrift, lost souls crowned with the tousled hair of palm trees in the wind. Try it" (14; 20). Clamence's whole discourse is a continual enticement for his companion to want to learn more.

The opening of the second chapter once again whets his companion's appetite. Clamence says, "What is a judge-penitent? Ah, I intrigued you with that little matter" (15; 21), thus confirming his explicitly expressed curiosity in this regard. The fact that Clamence regularly comes back to his role as judge-penitent to remind his interlocutor of his chosen profession serves as a kind of carrot to feed his companion's interest in what he has to say, just as it also serves to draw the reader on, ever further, in his quest to learn the secret of this strange profession for which Clamence has sacrificed his career as a lawyer. Note, too, that the *Monsieur* (5; 7) of the opening sentence of the novel had become *Monsieur et cher compatriote* (13; 19) by the end of the first chapter and is now replaced by *cher Monsieur* (16; 23).

We mentioned earlier that the manner in which Clamence illustrates what he calls his "vocation for summits" (21; 29) may well not ring completely true for his companion. There is something too systematic and methodical about his enumeration of all the different kinds of lofty situations he takes delight in and all those lowly, down-to-earth, even subterranean ones he avoids like the plague: "Coal-bunkers, ship-holds, subways, grottoes, pits were repulsive to me. I had even developed a special loathing for speleologists" (20; 29). This list reads almost like a definition lifted from a dictionary. His companion, however, doubtless puts this down to a tendency to exaggerate or, at worst, to a certain poetic license that passes for eloquence in the mouth of any lawyer. After all, Clamence shortly owns up to just such a tendency: "Anyway, I am perhaps exaggerating. I was at ease in everything, to be sure, but at the same time satisfied with nothing" (24; 34).

Clamence suddenly becomes aware of the need to renew their drinks, saying, "Allow me to call on our friend the primate." Once they are served, he tells his companion, "Nod your head to thank him and, above all, drink up with me, I need your understanding" (24; 35). And so, for the first time, he directly solicits the other's understanding. One can appreciate that he is a little taken aback by this appeal for understanding, which nothing could have led him to anticipate: "I see that this declaration amazes you" (24; 35). Moreover, Clamence reiterates his request by asking, "Have you never sudddenly needed understanding, help, friendship? Yes, of course"—and his companion has no reason to remain deaf to his plea. On the contrary, he has every reason, at this stage of their conversation, to be responsive and to feel sympathetic to such a request, particularly when Clamence adds that he has learned "to be satisfied with understanding." Decidedly, he is not asking for much in the circumstances.

He soon utters a no less poignant plea in the form of one of many rhetorical questions. After speaking of "a man whose friend had been imprisoned and who slept on the floor of his room every night in order not to enjoy a comfort of which his friend had been deprived," he asks, "Who, *cher* Monsieur, will sleep on the floor for us?" (25; 36), thereby subtly suggesting that in some way there are certain attributes they have in common.

It is not until the next chapter that Clamence again appeals to his companion. He is picturing the situation where everybody would have visiting cards and shop signs indicating their real, as opposed to their professed, identity: "Just fancy visiting cards: Dupont, jittery philosopher, or Christian landowner, or adulterous humanist. . . . But it would be hell! Yes, hell must be like that: streets filled with shop-signs and no way of explaining oneself. One is classified once and for all" (36; 52). Having formulated this eloquent diatribe against social and professional identities, Clamence turns to his companion to ask, "You, for instance, *mon cher compatriote*, stop and think of what your sign would be. You are silent? Well, you'll tell me later on." And in order to encourage him to embark upon a similar process of self-scrutiny, he volunteers his own answer: "I know mine in any case: a double face, a charming Janus, and above it the motto of the house: 'Don't rely on it'" (36; 52). Here his interlocutor is clearly called upon to follow Clamence's example. The suggestion is that having responded to the invitation, he will then have every reason to empathize with the speaker's process of self-discovery. This is the first time that he is explicitly invited to put himself in Clamence's shoes.

Clamence then goes on to describe the results of his soul-searching, which led to the recovery of his memory and his seeing and learning "by gradual degrees . . . a little of what [he] knew" (38; 54). "But before telling you of it," he says, "allow me, *mon cher compatriote*, to give you a few examples (they will be useful to you, I am sure) of what I discovered in the course of my exploration" (39; 56). This constitutes a further encouragement to follow the example set by the judge-penitent. And by this point, his companion is no doubt already anticipating that the results of his own search are not likely to be any more blameless than those illustrated by Clamence's anecdotes.

After recounting his exploits with the fair sex and the way in which he had managed to exploit his partners for his own sadistic satisfaction, he responds to what he takes to be his companion's disapproval: "I'll agree with you, though you politely haven't said a word, that that adventure is not a very pretty one." He adopts the same tactic as before, but his companion may well feel that he is becoming distinctly more insistent: "But just think of your life, *mon cher compatriote*! Search your memory and perhaps you will find some similar story that you'll tell me later on" (49; 70). He is now being incited in no uncertain terms to identify with Clamence. He is being told, in fact, that he has every reason to do so if he stops for a moment to think about it. He has probably, by this time, begun to feel some sympathy for Clamence's predicament, for he cannot but have been impressed by both his newfound lucidity and his complete honesty with himself, not to mention his frankness in relating what he has discovered about his past, euphoric existence. But empathy no longer suffices: now, he is being called upon actually to identify with Clamence by acknowledging that when all is said and done, there is no difference between them. Clamence's companion may well be saying to himself, "There but for the grace of God go I."

The beginning of the fourth chapter marks a further shift toward an even greater degree of attachment in the way Clamence addresses his companion. *Mon cher compatriote* now becomes quite simply *cher ami* (57; 77). And *attachment* is the appropriate term, for Clamence is continually building upon the ever-increasing feeling of complicity and identification he senses in his silent companion. As he says, he has "no more friends," only accomplices, which, by way of compensation, comprise "the whole human race": "And within the human race, you first of all" (55; 79). Thus, he is now laying claim to the friendship of this casual acquaintance, come upon by chance in the bar Mexico City. In fact, when he observes, after pointing out that one's suicide will always be misinterpreted to one's disadvantage, that "martyrs, *cher ami*, must choose between being forgotten, mocked, or made use of. As for being understood—never!" (56; 81), it is as though he expects to hear his companion protest that he at least has come some significant way toward understanding Clamence. If that is so, however, he is disappointed—for the moment at least—since no such words cross his companion's lips.

In the same chapter, Clamence interjects more and more, within his recounting of the events of his past life, questions addressed to his listener and references to the latter that serve to remind us of his continued presence. Sometimes the questions do not call for an answer of any kind: "After all I have told you, what do you think I developed? An aversion for myself? Come, come, it was mostly with others that I was fed up" (57; 81); or "They all strive to be rich. Why? Did you ever ask yourself? For power of course" (61; 87). They can be merely rhetorical questions: "Didn't I once go so far as to consider falsifying a friend's calendar?" (63; 90). At other times, they solicit a reaction that is not forthcoming. Whether or not his interlocutor is prepared to respond, Clamence merely presses on with his narrative: "The prosecution of others, on the contrary, went on constantly in my heart. Of course—does that shock you? Maybe you think it's not logical" (57; 81). Then there are what the linguists refer to as "phatic remarks," the function of which is to maintain contact with the other person, such as "If you doubt this . . ." (57; 82), "As I told you . . ." (61; 87), or "As you well imagine . . ." (66; 95). Even the first-person plural of the imperative verb can create a certain sense of complicity: "Besides, let's not beat about the bush; I love life . . ." (56; 81).

But gradually he manages to elicit a response from his listener. When the latter answers in the affirmative the question as to whether he knows Dante, Clamence pursues his reference to the Italian writer: "We are in the vestibule [of Hell], *cher ami*." And it is clear that his companion makes a comment: "Patience? You are probably right" (62; 89). The response is not always verbal, for having said that he has discovered at last that he was not so simple, Clamence adds, "Don't smile; that truth is not so fundamental as it seems" (62; 89), from which it is possible to deduce the reason for his companion's smile: Clamence's observation appears self-evident to him. Toward the end of the chapter, his listener clearly becomes more animated or at least more responsive. At one point, Clamence remarks, doubtless because of his listener's reaction, "You must find all that childish" (68; 99). A little later, Clamence's discourse clearly registers a reaction from his companion: "The amazement I generally encountered in my listeners, their rather reticent embarrassment, somewhat like what you are showing—no, don't protest—did not calm me at all" (70; 101). His "reticent embarrassment" is of course significant, since it reveals that in spite of Clamence's many different strategies to create a sense of complicity—appeals to his culture, his intelligence, his sense of humor, as well as Clamence's repeated questions seeking confirmation of, and concurrence with, the points he is making—his companion is still far from being completely won over.

There is no doubt that there is a strategy at work here, for he remarks at one point, "I stop there, for too great a symmetry would upset my argument" (63; 91). This statement recalls a similar symmetry that characterized his enumeration of the heights he loves and the depths he despises. Such a remark could warn his listener that there is more going on here than meets the eye. But evidently, if it strikes his companion at all, he soon dismisses it or simply attributes it to Clamence's need to give a clear account of his own evolution. Even if he is yet to be won over to Clamence's point of view, there is no doubt that by now his interest and curiosity have been fully aroused: "No, I interest you? You are very polite." Clamence is keen to nurture this interest: "Moreover, I now run the risk of really interesting you. Before explaining myself on the subject of judges-penitent, I must talk to you of debauchery and of the little-ease" (71; 102). And so ends the fourth chapter, with the main source of his listener's curiosity being skillfully sustained by a delaying tactic that is pursued right up until the sixth and last chapter of the novel.

The next, penultimate chapter adds little to the devices that Clamence employs in his attempt to develop a rapport with his listener. There are more of the same questions, rhetorical and otherwise, and the same asides to assure himself of his listener's continued attention and interest. *Cher ami* has now been replaced by the even more intimate *cher* (72; 103) and *mon cher* (72; 104), with which it will alternate before becoming simply *mon ami* (87; 125) by the last sentence of the chapter. As he did earlier, he gives the impression of letting himself get carried away by his own eloquence, appealing to his listener to help him curb his flights of language: "I am becoming lyrical! Stop me, *mon cher*, I beg you" (72; 104). His description of how, in Greece, virile-looking men stride along hand in hand is not without significance, for it leads him to ask his companion, "But tell me, would you take my hand in the streets of Paris?" He immediately adds, "Oh, I'm joking. *We* have a sense of decorum" (73; 104). His listener's curiosity is rekindled every time Clamence introduces into his narrative a remark the meaning of which he is unable to grasp, as when he says, "I interrupted myself, I believe, on the way to the little-ease." He immediately seeks an explanation, as Clamence's words reveal: "Yes, I'll tell you what I mean" (73; 104). When he says of one of his mistresses that she talked of love with the "conviction of an intellectual announcing the classless society" and adds that "such conviction, as you must know, is contagious" (74; 106), he knows of what he speaks, since he is obviously banking on the fact that his companion finds the conviction of his own elegant discourse and finely tuned arguments no less compelling.

Militating in Clamence's favor is not only the lucidity he displays in analyzing his conduct but also his frankness. "Dare I admit it to you?" (76; 109), he interjects at one point, and then immediately proceeds to make the admission in question, although not without adding another, less reassuring opinion: "Truth . . . is a colossal bore" (75; 108). In other words, he gives his listener the distinct impression that he is confiding in him by letting him into certain secrets: "I'll reveal this secret to you, *cher ami*, don't be afraid to make use of it" (76; 109). And what exactly is the "secret"? Merely that alcohol and women provided him with the only solace he was worthy of. Another "big secret" he refers to a little later is no less of a letdown, since it is no more personal and private than many of the maxims that serve to pad out his apparent "confession": "I'll tell you a big secret, *mon cher*. Don't wait for the Last Judgement. It takes place every day" (82; 118).

Yet again he apologizes for letting himself get carried away and resorting to his old habits as a lawyer: "I'm on the point of making a speech to the court. Forgive me and realize that I have my reasons" (85; 121). But now it would seem that appearances are indeed deceptive, just as sheer silk can conceal eczema. What those reasons are is not, however, elaborated upon, so why should his listener feel any cause for concern? In fact, by the end of this chapter, Clamence feels confident enough of the success of his well-honed powers of persuasion to affirm: "You have had a chance to observe that I spare nothing and, as for you, I know that you think as I do" (86; 123). And the tantalizing reminder of his role as judge-penitent is evoked only to be immediately put off as a topic of discussion until the morrow.

With the opening of the final chapter—in which *mon cher* now alternates with the even more intimate form of address *très cher* (97; 140), representing the culmination of an ever-increasing degree of complicity—Clamence's discourse takes a distinctly disquieting turn for his interlocutor. The expresson on his companion's face provokes a reaction: "I know what you're thinking: it's very hard to disentangle the true from the false in what I'm saying. I admit you are right. I myself . . ." (88; 127). Did he not say earlier that he considered truth a bore? Moreover, between the countless anecdotes he has been telling and the maxims he has been formulating, the very possibility of distinguishing between truth and falsehood becomes blurred: anecdotes, like any other tale, have, after all, much in common with fiction, and maxims, inasmuch as they are generalizations, are both true and false, thus sharing the ambiguous status of literature itself.

He then goes on to create a far more disturbing situation, the specter of deliberate, concerted lying and concealment. Clamence proposes three alternatives to describe himself: "Those who prefer having nothing to hide rather than being obliged to lie, those who prefer lying to having nothing to hide, and finally those who like both lying and the hidden" (88; 127). Now only the first category of person does not lie consciously and has nothing to hide, but even so feels a compulsion to lie. That the speaker considers a propensity for dissimulation to characterize the whole human race must tell us something about his own truthfulness—particularly since he goes out of his way to include himself within the three categories: "I'll let you choose which case suits me best" (88; 127). What is even more important here is that his listener is being called upon to decide for himself to which of the three classes of people Clamence belongs. In other words, he is being compelled to ask himself whether or not Clamence is an inveterate liar, knowing full well that he is a compulsive speaker. And in order to be able to ramble on endlessly as Clamence has appeared to be doing, does one not sooner or later have to invent things, as well as indulge in exaggeration—an activity he has already confessed to?

Here, for the first time during their one-sided conversation, Clamence is throwing the ball into his interlocutor's court by asking him a question he cannot evade, since it concerns his own attitude toward all that Clamence has been telling him so insistently and persistently. In short, his companion now finds himself irremediably implicated in the situation that has gradually been developing since the evening Clamence first drew up his glass beside his own in the bar Mexico City.

What the judge-penitent goes on to add is in no way likely to set his companion's mind to rest: "But what do I care? Don't lies eventually lead to the truth? And don't all my stories, true or false, tend towards the same conclusion? Don't they all have the same meaning? So what does it matter whether they are true or false if, in both cases, they are significant of what I am?" (88; 128). Clamence's companion must now confront the meaning of that "same conclusion." That the outcome of his marathon listening sessions will be no different whether Clamence has been speaking the truth or lying must provoke the listener into asking himself what has been and what is, in fact, the point of Clamence's monologue. Why has the erstwhile lawyer chosen to buttonhole him and refused to let him go? The very use of the term *stories*, which more often than not serves to designate a fictional or imaginary account of some kind, must already give his companion pause.

The interlocutor may feel reasonably sure of at least one thing: what he has been listening to is intended to be, in some sense, significant of what Clamence has been and what he is. But in what sense exactly? And if Clamence believes, as he goes on to say, that sometimes "it is easier to see clearly into the liar than into the man who tells the truth" (88; 128), does this not suggest that he is indeed likely to be lying? Once again, the onus of deciding the truth of the matter is placed squarely on his companion's shoulders: "Well, take it how you like . . ." (88, 128).

Soon the question arises as to what Clamence's underlying motivation has been in so confiding in his companion. He admits to a pronounced penchant for confessions of any kind: "At any rate, I have ceased to like anything but confessions, and authors of confessions write especially to avoid confessing, to tell nothing of what they know. When they claim to get to the painful admissions, you have to watch out, for they are about to dress the corpse" (89; 128–29). The warning could not be clearer, and just in case his listener has missed the point and failed to make the connection with his own situation, Clamence drives the point home: "Believe me, I know what I am talking about" (89; 129). The name he has given to the new vocation he has devised for himself inevitably comes to mind. His previous remarks have already illustrated his ambivalent attitude to the judge's function; now, his listener has begun to realize that his role as penitent is no less ambivalent.

Understandably, his companion now becomes even more attentive. As Clamence informs him that he was "named Pope in a prison-camp" (88; 128), his listener is eager to learn more about the circumstances of such an extraordinary event and so brings him back to the topic in question: "You are curious to know my pontifical adventures?" (89; 129). Soon he has the impression that for his taste, Clamence is progressing too quickly in the telling of his tale and missing out details that may be very important: "I can see from your manner that I am skipping rather fast, in your opinion, over these details which have a certain significance" (90–91; 131). In any case, before long, the question of the veracity of this account of his past life in North Africa during the war arises in this new context. The mention of a young Frenchman in the camp being a believer in God provokes this rejoinder: "Yes, it's decidedly a fairy-tale!" (91; 132). Perhaps this, too, is a fairy tale, just like the innumerable tales and anecdotes that have preceded it, says the listener to himself.

Finally, Clamence returns to the topic of his present profession, saying that since his companion is on the point of leaving, "it is time . . . for me to tell you what it is" (96; 139). He points out that he is already practicing it at the very moment he is speaking. His companion learns for the first time that he is himself a client of the judge-penitent and indeed has been from the very beginning of their conversation together: "Don't get the idea that I have talked to you at such length for five days just for the fun of it" (96; 139). There is a point, then, to Clamence's insistent monologue. There is nothing random about Clamence's apparent rambling-on: "My words have a purpose. They have the purpose, obviously, of silencing the laughter, of avoiding judgement personally . . ." (96; 139). His listener suddenly realizes that it is he himself who is personally at risk when Clamence adds ominously that since "we are the first to condemn ourselves . . . it is essential to begin by extending the condemnation to all, without distinction": "No excuses ever, for anyone; that's my principle at the outset" (96; 139–40). The judge has now taken the place of the penitent, and in front of him sits the man who has lent him his undivided attention and sympathetic understanding. After further digressions, the judge-penitent finally explains exactly what it is that he has been up to over the previous five days:

> [My useful profession] consists to begin with, as you know from experience, in indulging in public confession as often as possible. I accuse myself up hill and down dale. . . . But let me point out that I don't accuse myself crudely, beating my breast. No, I navigate skilfully, multiplying distinctions and digressions too—in short I adapt my words to my listener and lead him to go me one better. I mingle what concerns me and what concerns others, I choose the features we have in common, the experiences we have endured together, the failings we share. . . . With all that I construct a portrait which is the image of all and of no one. A mask, in short, rather like those carnival masks which are both lifelike and stylized so that they make people say: "Why, surely I've met him!" When the portrait is finished, as it is this evening, I show it with great sorrow: "This, alas, is what I am!" The prosecutor's

charge is finished. But at the same time the portrait that I hold out
to my contemporaries becomes a mirror. (102; 147–48)

And so, by dint of empathizing with what he had taken to be
Clamence's life story, drawn on into an ever-closer complicity with
this cultured, perspicacious, and witty commentator on contemporary
society, he has come to the point of identifying with, and thereby
assuming, those very character weaknesses that the lucid and uncom-
promisingly self-critical storyteller has been condemning. As for
Clamence's own transformation from repentant penitent to accusing
judge, he explains the transition thus: "I stand before all humanity . . .
saying: 'I was the lowest of the low.' Then imperceptibly I pass from
the 'I' to the 'we.' When I get to 'This is what we are,' the game is
over . . ." (102–3; 148). But not quite, for the more he accuses himself,
the more he has the right to judge the other person. As he puts it,
"Even better, I provoke you into judging yourself."

What he seeks, then, is not to have to rely on his own condemnation of his interlocutor but rather to be able to count on the latter's
own self-condemnation: "If we merely look back over our lives, there's
no lack of occasions to amaze and scandalize ourselves. Just try. I shall
listen, you may be sure, to your own confession with a great feeling of
fraternity" (103; 149). Clamence's companion has now had the tables
turned on him completely: he had thought that his capacity for sympathy and understanding of another's sad experiences was being solicit-
ed, whereas he now discovers, to his dismay, that it is he who is in
need of the other's compassion.

At this crucial juncture, Clamence says to him, "Don't laugh!"
But whether the judge-penitent is trying to forestall his laughter
because he is unsure of the reception his declaration will receive or
whether, on the contrary, his companion did actually laugh, we cannot
be sure. And if he did laugh, how are we to interpret his laugh? What
is there, in fact, to laugh at? Perhaps he finds the speaker amusing in
his earnestness, or again perhaps he finds his explanations quite
implausible. His laugh could even be a nervous laugh giving expression
to a certain apprehensiveness. The possibilities are numerous because
the significance of his laughing at this precise moment, after

Clamence's unexpected revelation of how he has manipulated and duped his listener right from their very first meeting, is far from clear. What is more, how we interpret this moment in the novel will play a pivotal role in our interpretation of the whole work. The key question is whether or not his companion, in the final analysis, finds Clamence convincing.

At this point, the would-be judge-penitent senses or suspects some resistance, for he goes on to say, "Yes, you are a difficult client; I saw that at once," while at the same time appearing to remain sure of himself and certain of winning over his interlocutor: "But you'll come to it inevitably" (103; 149). But then again, how sure of himself is he really?

Once more, he resorts to flattery in order to overcome any remaining resistance: "Most of the others are more sentimental than intelligent; they are disconcerted at once. . . . *You* are not only intelligent, you looked polished by use," which suggests that his companion has not, for the moment, revealed himself to be "disconcerted" by Clamence's exposition, let alone bowled over by it. "With the intelligent ones it takes time. It is enough to explain the method fully to them. They don't forget it; they reflect. Sooner or later, half as a game, and half out of emotional upset, they give up and tell all" (103; 149), he adds confidently. In other words, he does not necessarily count on immediate success and is content to be faced with a waiting game. He is patient, and once the process is well under way, like a termite in the woodwork, it is only a question of time: "Admit, however, that today you feel less pleased with yourself than you felt five days ago? Now I shall wait for you to write to me or to come back. For you will come back, I am sure!" (103; 149). There seems no place for any element of uncertainty in the judge-penitent's mind; he clearly has complete confidence in the ultimate success of his method, of which the outcome, however long it is in coming, is assured in advance. "So I shall await your respects at *Mexico City* as long as necessary" (104; 150–51).

By now, Clamence admits to feeling "a sort of affection" (104; 151) for his latest client, a demonstration of his own assertion that accomplices in guilt can indeed substitute for friends in the normal sense of the term. For himself, however, he confesses that his "solution is not the ideal" (106; 152–53). The vehemence, noted earlier, with which he insists that he is really happy at last would seem to suggest as much: "I am happy I tell you, I won't let you think I'm not happy" (105; 152).

As for his companion, he apparently becomes agitated when Clamence suggests that the descent of the doves in the guise of snowflakes heralds everyone's salvation and that his companion will sleep every night on the ground for him (as though in response to his earlier question, "Who, *cher* Monsieur, will sleep on the floor for us?" [25; 36]): "All right, all right, I'll be quiet; don't get upset!" (106; 154). Again, the significance of his sudden agitation is unclear. And right up to the end of the novel, the ambiguity concerning his companion's attitude and response to the confession turned accusation remains intact: "Why, now that you are going to talk to me about yourself, I shall find out whether or not one of the objectives of my absorbing confession is achieved" (107; 154). The reader is thus, it appears, in the same situation as Clamence himself—in other words, none the wiser. Within the world of the fiction, however, the judge-penitent expects to discover someday the effect he has finally achieved, but the reader will never know.

In the final pages of the text, the author introduces a piece of information about Clamence's companion that will turn out to be crucial for the interpretation of this novel. It concerns his profession: "But of course you are not a policeman; that would be too easy. What? Ah, I suspected as much, you see. So that strange affection I felt for you had sense to it. You practise in Paris the noble profession of lawyer!" (107; 155). This comes as quite a shock to the reader. Later I shall have occasion to return to this final twist in the tale to examine in detail its implications.

9

The Role of the Reader

Over the last few years, students of literature have been made more and more aware by critics and literary theorists that all novels imply the presence of a reader. On one level, this fact is self-evident in that all writing of any kind, literary or otherwise, is clearly intended to be read. Less obvious is the fact that novels in particular not only offer themselves up for reading but also play an active role in determining the manner in which they will be read. To point out that they give us, as readers, guidance in our job of making sense of them may appear to be equally self-evident; by the same token, they also provide the means for our eliminating inappropriate strategies of interpretation.

It is possible to construct the portrait of a certain kind of reader from the sum total of indications provided by the novel to guide us in our understanding of what we are reading. The exact nature of the guidelines provided, both the amount and type of information—psychological, sociological, philosophical, etc.— presupposes and implies that the reader possesses certain definable characteristics in that he or she is more or less knowledgeable about certain things. This means that the texts of all novels have written into them a particular kind of implied reader, before they even come to be read by any actual reader.

It should be added that since such a reader is only implied, he or she is not, by definition, addressed in person through the second-person pronoun; if the reader were so addressed, his or her presence would of course become explicit.

To return now to *The Fall*, Camus's novel is narrated in the first person, and the first person always implies the accompanying presence of a second person, and vice versa. For the narrator to designate himself or herself as *I*, there has to be, potentially at least, a second person to whom he or she is telling the story in question. The two personal pronouns are in fact interdependent. In the case of *The Fall*, however, the second person, far from possessing the characteristics of an implied addressee, is explicitly designated by the second-person pronoun *you*. What we have here in effect is a hybrid narrative situation, a cross between a first- and second-person narrative, since while he is explicitly addressed and his presence thereby evoked, the second person in question, Clamence's listener, is hardly ever directly depicted by the text of the novel, except in the most fleeting and general terms, quite inadequate to the task of characterizing him as a person.

A further and equally significant distinction needs to be drawn here: this implied addressee is not, of course, an implied reader but an implied listener. What he does share with the implied reader is the fact that his presence is merely implied. He, like any implied reader, is programmed into the text, his every reaction being determined by Clamence's monologue.

It is important to appreciate the pertinence of the concept of the implied reader in understanding how the text of *The Fall* functions. The writing into the text of an implied listener lacking any explicit, clearly defined novelistic identity brings into being a very particular type of implied reader, for it is the reader who will feel himself or herself incited to provide the shadowy listener with an identity and fill in the empty form of the person being addressed by Clamence. That identity will be none other than his or her own identity,[1] although the reader will not become aware of this fact until Clamence's revelation in the last chapter. It is in this way that Clamence's implied listener comes to shade off into and finally merge with an implied reader of *The Fall* and that an explicit addressee paradoxically yields to, and makes way for, an implicit addressee. This explains how the text of this novel engages and implicates its reader in such an exceptionally complex and original fashion. This development is made possible by the presence of the second-person pronoun, and its potentiality as a shifter—that is, a part of speech the meaning of which is determined solely by the circumstances in which it is employed—is here cleverly exploited. The resulting subtle ambiguity effects a shift within the addressee, so that in the final analysis, on the level of the work's reception—and on that level alone—Clamence's companion becomes Camus's reader. I will now examine in detail how this process is activated.

As noted in the previous chapter, there is no identifiable person sitting in the spot occupied by Clamence's addressee. His companion does not enjoy the status of a fictional character worthy of the name. Inasmuch as he exists at all, it is as a kind of empty slot in the text—an empty space made up of all the empty spaces between Clamence's utterances—whose occupant is nonetheless implied by the dialogical situation the monologue refers to. In other words, in the spot pointed to by Clamence's words, there is a void. Now, the property of any void or vacuum is that it inevitably tends to implode upon itself, drawing into its center all that surrounds it. As noted earlier, the shadowy presence of Clamence's listener hovers not in the background but in the foreground, and that distinction of location here proves crucial: he is situated on this side of Clamence, that is, between Clamence and the reader, coming between the two of them. It is as though the reader were looking over the listener's shoulder and, hence, as though Clamence were addressing the reader directly over that same shoulder.

It is this particular situation that confers upon *The Fall*, from its opening pages, a uniquely open-ended structure—with its open-endedness pointing toward the reader, thanks to the existence of that empty space delimiting the situation of Clamence's companion. It is the fact that *The Fall* is also a second-person, as well as a first-person, narrative that brings about this exceptional state of affairs and formally distinguishes this work from virtually any other novel. The second-person pronoun shares with the first-person pronoun its linguistic status as a shifter, by its very nature and function a kind of empty slot, which, unlike a third-person pronoun, is dependent for its meaning on the dialogical situation in which it happens to be uttered. The *I*, of course, always refers to whoever happens to be speaking at a given moment, and the *you*, to whomever he happens to be speaking to. Thus, the meaning of each potentially shifts every time it is uttered. Since the first-person pronoun is constant in *The Fall*, it always, without exception, refers to Clamence. It is the relatively unidentified and unidentifiable second person whose virtuality waits to be activated. That it calls to be filled in, just like any other void, ensures that the space it marks out lies, in relation to the reader, in front of, rather than behind, Clamence, thus creating an open-ended structure that, of necessity, points away from where Clamence is sitting and speaking, outside of the text of his monologue and hence toward his unheard and unseen listener and beyond, toward the reader.

The only possible closure in the case of a text that opens up toward the outside is one brought about by the very act of reading. It is the reader who will come to complete this incomplete structure. All that is needed for this end to be attained and for *The Fall*'s preordained destiny to be realized is the mere presence of a reader reading. In this respect, through its formal structure, Camus's novel can be seen to be emblematic of a process synonymous with all literary activity of any kind, given that no literary work comes to fruition until it is read: until that moment, it does no more than subsist in a state of limbo as an unread text, awaiting its reader to bring it to life as a fictional universe in his or her mind's eye (Fitch, 1991).

What I am concerned with here is not, in the first instance at least, a process of identification by which the reader comes to identify with Clamence's listener; indeed, there is nothing for him or her to identify with. Or to put it another way, if the reader were to identify with Clamence's companion, this would certainly not entail exchanging his or her own identity for that of another—a very important point as far as the outcome of the reading of the novel is concerned. The text calls upon the reader to occupy the mere space or physical situation taken up by the listener. What is involved is a process of substitution rather than one of identification.

Another decisive factor instigating the reader to effect such a substitution was described in detail in the last chapter. It is the force of attraction that Clamence exerts on his listener, all those devices whereby he nurtures in his listener a sense of complicity by appealing to his sympathy and understanding and even going so far as to solicit his friendship. Now, he naturally exerts the same influence on the reader that he exerts on his interlocutor through the various human qualities he exhibits, such as his frankness, his complete honesty with himself, his newfound lucidity, and, last but not least, his relentless self-criticism. In short, the reader is subject to exactly the same force of attraction and fascination. There is no reason to believe that he or she is any less susceptible to the speaker's persistent efforts to create a rapport through his manipulative monologue than is Clamence's listener.

What results is a kind of piggyback effect. As Clamence's listener is gradually drawn into an ever-greater feeling of complicity with the speaker, the reader cannot but follow his lead. The image of somebody riding piggyback on another comes to mind because the force of attraction exerted by Clamence is preceded, and subsequently complemented, by that quite different force of attraction exerted by the empty void marking the spot where his unheard companion is sitting. In other words, as the reader is being drawn toward the listener in the sense of gradually and imperceptibly taking over his position in front of the voluble Clamence, the listener is being no less gradually and imperceptibly drawn toward Clamence through his increasing sympathy for, and empathy with, the apparent penitent. The movement of the reader outside of himself or herself thus gathers momentum, opening up the world of the fiction. This dual force of attraction cannot fail to implicate the reader in the text being read. The reader is conscious of becoming caught up in the situation he or she had sat back to contemplate at a safe aesthetic distance.

The process by which the reader is taken up by, and implicated in, the fictional universe is a gradual one. It naturally gains momentum as the various sessions of monologue-cum-conversation succeed one another. The direct questions Clamence puts to his listener clearly accelerate the evolution of the relationship that develops between the reader and the work. When he remarks, for example, "Stop and think what your sign would be," where the imperative form of the verb functions as an interrogative, it is important to note that no answer is forthcoming: "You're silent? Well, you'll tell me later on" (36; 52). Or again, when he enjoins his listener, "But just think of your life, *mon cher compatriote*. Search your memory and perhaps you will find some similar story that you'll tell me later on" (49; 70). The fact that such injunctions remain without any explicit response is highly significant, for the absence of any response opens up yet another gap in the text that will, in its turn, exert its power of attraction on the reader. If his companion were to reply, then the reader would have no difficulty in distancing himself from that reply, that is, registering it while quite naturally attributing it to the character uttering it and to him alone. As it is, there is nothing that stands between Clamence's injunction and implied question, on the one hand, and the reader, on the other hand, so the reader is subjected to their full impact. The text is here set up and devised by its author in such a way that it appears to be saying to the reader, If the shoe fits, wear it!

The interplay between reader and textual void goes one decisive stage further, however. The empty slot provided by the shifter, the second-person pronoun *you*, is finally subsumed within an even more radical hollowing out of the text, which will leave the reader trapped in an uncomfortable situation. The object of this hollowing out and voiding of substance is none other than the character of Clamence himself.

Before mapping out this final decisive development, it is important to stress what emerged from the detailed analysis of the reactions of Clamence's companion in the previous chapter: his reactions, for lack of an omniscient narrator, were never made explicit, so their precise nature and hence their significance remain unclear. Witness our attempts to interpret the listener's laugh. Whether or not the listener's reactions are ambiguous to Clamence, within the fictional reality of the book's universe, is not germane to the point being made. Any human behavior viewed from outside, by another, is potentially, to some extent, ambiguous, and it would take an omniscient third-person narrator to resolve that ambiguity.

Now the fact that the unseen listener's reactions are of an ambiguous character throws significant light on a key feature of this work discussed at the beginning of the present chapter, the manner in which it programs its own reading. While there are no clearly identified reactions to Clamence's words depicted—however indirectly—to come between the reader and his own reactions, there is nonetheless clear evidence that the monologue is indeed reacted to. Thus, the text does not allow for the monologue to be received passively, with an attitude of mere indifference. Not only is reaction called for, but it is clearly called forth because evidence of such reaction is inscribed in the text itself. What all this adds up to is a text that, through its formal structure and its hybrid first-and-second-person narrative, programs its own reception without predetermining what that reception will be. The phenomenon could not be more paradoxical, which perhaps explains why criticism devoted to this novel contains no precise analysis of what is involved here. The subtle and shifting interplay between the two parallel situations—Clamence's companion listening and responding to his monologue and the reader reading and responding to *The Fall*—ensures that the reader is not allowed to remain indifferent to the insistent barrage of words and yet is left free to react to it as he or she thinks fit (one is tempted to add, as best he or she can). This feature of the text will prove crucial to our understanding of its ultimate impact upon the reader. It also explains the title given to the present chapter, for it is clear that the reader has here a role mapped out for him or her, although since the precise content of that role is not predetermined, it would be more apposite to speak of a "function" rather than of a "role."

Let us now examine how the character of the narrator-protagonist becomes hollowed out, how Clamence comes to disintegrate before our very eyes. This crucial development occurs in the very last chapter of the novel. As he lies in bed to receive his visitor for the last time, Clamence greets him with the most disconcerting remarks to date when he sets about dividing up humanity into three categories, all revealing the same propensity for lying, and after having agreed that it is "very hard to disentangle the true from the false" (88; 127) in what he is saying. He adds that whether his stories are true or false is of no importance, since they are all indicative of what he is and has been. He then goes on to point out that he knows what he is talking about in claiming that all authors of confessions "write especially to avoid confessing" and "to tell nothing of what they know" (89; 128–29). This raises in the reader's mind the distinct possibility that Clamence has been lying all along and that the tale of his past life is a complete and utter fabrication. It brings to mind some of Clamence's previous asides, such as his remark that "too great a symmetry would upset [his] argument" (63; 91), and his endless enumeration of all those heights he loved and those depths he detested. The fact that he explicitly attributed to himself "a double face, a charming Janus" (36; 52) suddenly takes on a new significance. In light of these remarks, what is the reader to believe? Is there any truth in what Clamence has been saying in the previous days' monologues?

The reader next discovers that when he was in a prisoner-of-war camp, Clamence "had another name" (92; 133), one other than Jean-Baptiste. And so he has assumed a new identity, that of "Jean-Baptiste Clamence," expressly for the purposes of his new profession of judge-penitent. His assuming a new identity reminds the reader that he admitted that he "used to act in plays" (65; 93). In fact his love of playacting was such that he suggested his visiting card should read, "Jean-Baptiste Clamence, play-actor" (36; 52). It is now apparent, however, that Jean-Baptiste Clamence is not the name of the actor but, on the contrary, that of the role he has been playing!

The possibility that the judge-penitent has been lying from the outset rapidly becomes a probability with the revelation that his whole monologue has indeed been a fabrication, in the strictest sense of the term, wherein a portrait has been constructed "which is the image of all and no one": "A mask, in short [to] make people say: 'Why surely I've met him!'" (102; 148). Now for the first time the reader can appreciate why the judge-penitent's monologue has been peppered with so many maxims. What better means for creating a portrait "of all and no one" than the general truths embodied in maxims?

At this point in the novel, the whole of the substance of the preceding monologue goes up in smoke, dissipating into thin air, just like an illusion performed on the stage by a conjurer. And the character of Jean-Baptiste Clamence collapses with it, for what does the reader know of him now? It is true that the reader cannot be sure that there is not a single word of truth in what he or she has been listening to for so long (for readers, too, listen to that inner voice produced by their reading). Once the seed of doubt is sown in the mind, however, it cannot fail to germinate, just as it had done in the mind of a certain former Parisian lawyer—or so the reader has been led to believe. This doubt then proceeds to gnaw into Clamence's very substance as a character, revealing it to be doubly fictitious: what was previously taken to be a fictional character has proved to be the figment of another character's imagination—a fiction within a fiction. The doubt leaves in its wake yet another yawning gap in the text. And once again, this new textual void exerts its power of attraction, first of all on the judge-penitent's companion and then, through the latter, on the reader.

The attraction experienced is none other than that exerted by one's own reflection in a mirror, for this was the judge-penitent's expressed intention: "The portrait I hold out to my contemporaries becomes a mirror" (102; 148). And once again, it has been those universal truths expressed in the form of maxims that have possessed the generality necessary to bring about the transformation of a portrait of someone else into a mirror-image of oneself. This transformation captures exactly, in a single, strikingly evocative visual image, the transmutation of a confession into an accusation.

Thus, the text that began as open-ended and pointing toward its reader finally turns into a structure lacking any definite and final closure; the text appears to disintegrate into nothingness, or rather it calls upon its reader for completion, here to be understood in a rather particular sense.

The completion the reader brings to the work is itself not an act of definitive closure: the reader is called upon to take up where the judge-penitent's revelation of the raison d'être of his monologue left off and is thereby left to his or her own devices. And among those devices, self-scrutiny and self-interpretation will be paramount. Each and every reader of *The Fall* will provide not an ending to an unfinished novel but his or her own personal continuation to the mechanism of self-doubt that the work has set in motion. It is up to the reader whether the evolution of this gnawing self-doubt is ever to come to rest. In this sense, then, the open-endedness of the work remains intact, its disturbing resonances echoing potentially without end in the consciousness of its reader. Thus, Camus's work takes its rightful place in the long tradition of French *moralistes* stretching back to the sixteenth century.

Not everything disappears, however, once the veracity of the monologue is put in question. Here the important distinction between the two fictional worlds of the novel established in chapter 4 comes into play. What goes up in a puff of smoke is the substance of the world of the professedly former Parisian lawyer, that of the speaker's past life. The world of the bar Mexico City, on the other hand, remains as (fictionally) real as ever; and at the center of that world sits a character whose presence imposes itself upon the reader with even more immediacy. The reason the text insists on coming back, at the beginning and end of almost all the book's chapters, to what appears to be the mere setting or backdrop to the all-important monologue now becomes clear: it is to establish the reality and tangible presence of the storyteller as a counterweight to the story told. As the past recedes into the mists of a dubious fabulation, the present comes into the sharpest possible focus as the reader finds himself in the presence of someone who has, he declares, taken on the function of a judge-penitent, a function the bemused reader has no inclination to doubt. This presence has now taken on all the immediacy of an inescapable confrontation. The suddenly revealed insubstantiality of the events depicted in the story of the speaker's past life only serves to heighten the reality of the the reader's situation, the reality of the finger pointing at him or her in a gesture of accusation.

The situation in question bears a striking resemblance to what we encounter in the theater once the curtain has come down and the actor who has been playing the hero comes out in front of the curtain to take his bow.[2] The judge-penitent has now discarded the "mask" (102; 148) he has been wearing representing a certain Jean-Baptiste Clamence, and stands revealed as the actor whose performance has been holding us in its sway.

The leitmotive of the actor and playacting having already been noted, what remains to be examined is the theme of the mask complemented by the even more insistent theme of the double. The image of Janus, the presence of the Dutchmen both here and elsewhere, his living his past life under a double code, his present dual identity of judge-penitent—all these indices of duality and ambiguity can be seen to be the result of a psychologically split personality brought about by the speaker's indulging in endless self-interrogation and relentless introspection. They are now seen in a new light as they bring into focus the gap that separates the mask from its wearer, a gap that has opened up once and for all as the mask has fallen from its wearer's countenance.

By the end of a play, the theater audience feels it has come to know the character the portrayal of whom it has been following attentively from the first to the last act; that does not, of course, mean that it knows the actor who has been playing the part. On the contrary, the better the actor, the less the audience will know of him as a person. For the real-life person taking his bow before the audience has until that moment been completely concealed beneath the physiological and psychological features of the role he or she has been acting out. The situation of the reader at the end of *The Fall* is very much like that of the theater audience. In both cases, the final outcome of the theatrical performance marks a return to reality. The only difference, albeit a crucial one, is that here the actor is clearly more important than the role of Jean-Baptiste Clamence. No less than the playgoers getting up from their seats and leaving the theater, the reader of *The Fall* is brought back down to earth: in the reader's case, by the shock of the speaker's revelation of what he has really been up to all this time. The reader is then thrown back into a private, personal world where he or she has to face up to, and live with, his or her own foibles and moral shortcomings, rather than merely witnessing and being a party to those of another through the intermediary of theatrical illusion.

The image of the theater serves, above all, to highlight the extent to which the judge-penitent remains, or rather has suddenly become, for the reader, a completely unknown quantity. At the same time, it vividly evokes the inescapable immediacy of his presence before us. In the absence of any knowledge of the person in question, the reader is now confronted not by anything as abstract and intangible as a void but by the material presence of a stranger. This distinction is crucial once one recalls that the empty outline of the judge-penitent's interlocutor can easily be lost sight of by the reader in that it calls out for the reader to take his place. There is no longer an attraction-exerting textual vacuum but a stranger claiming and exhibiting all the characteristics of a judge and holding the reader at a distance by his insinuating accusations.

The exact extent and compass of his lies and fabrications are not known to the reader. Has he ever been a Parisian lawyer? Perhaps he was indeed a lawyer but has merely invented the rest of his autobiography. Then again, perhaps he did go through some form of moral crisis but in circumstances other than those he related. If the whole tale of his past life appears to be dubious, how serious is his commitment to his avowed profession of judge-penitent? This is not clear either. The reader does not know what to think of the person facing him or her.

This is, moreover, hardly the reader's main concern. All that matters now is that the other person is perceived as a threat, a threat to the reader's psychological well-being. The reader finds his attention directed inward, as all fictionality slips away from a situation that allows for no escape. Nothing could be more paradoxical than this final decisive turn of events whereby fictional reality has somehow encroached upon the existential reality of the reader (Fitch, 1991, 114–36)—not, it should be stressed, in his capacity as a reader but as a human being. Nothing, that is, except for the contiguity of the world of fiction and the real world that is found in any theater, where the edge of the stage constitutes the boundary between the realm of the imaginary and that of the real, live audience. With this final twist in the tale, the reader becomes a part of the problem enunciated and embroidered upon by the monologue being read, and hence part of the problem posed by the interpretation of *The Fall*.

10

Rereading and Interpreting *The Fall*

Camus once wrote of the novelist Franz Kafka that his works are intended to be reread (*Essais*, 201). The same may be justly said of Camus's own fiction and of *The Fall* in particular. The revelation coming at the end of its final chapter leaves the reader perplexed and puzzled, and he or she feels compelled to reread the novel to find out exactly where he or she went wrong and allowed the tables to be turned on him or her by the judge-penitent. Indeed, the reading of any novel may well be followed by rereadings to arrive at some kind of overall interpretation. In fact, from the end of the first reading onward, the reader inevitably yields once and for all to the interpreter. This distinction between reading and interpreting is particularly apposite in the case of Camus's last novel, although it is true that the very act of understanding what we read itself entails a form of interpretation.

My choosing to use *the reader* in the previous chapter rather than the first-person plural pronoun *we* to describe the reading of the novel was significant. The reader is directly implicated in this text, which clearly marks out the space he or she is to occupy. *The Fall* is manifestly designed by its author to entrap its reader, just as his character's monologue is devised so as to ensnare his companion. It must be stressed once again that while the way it is read is textually preordained, this is not true of the way it is reacted to. The reader's reactions remain his or her own. Nonetheless, it was precisely the degree to which "the reader" is programmed into the text that enables me to speak of him or her in those terms, generalizing about the reader's status and interaction with the text of the novel.

I will now turn from the actual process involved in reading *The Fall* to the results to be drawn from its reading. What is to be made of such a perturbing experience? Here it is appropriate to allow for a number of different and even contradictory interpretations of this work, since it does expressly leave room for any number of reactions to the judge-penitent's monologue. In other words, "the reader" referred to in the previous chapter is not synonymous with any actual reader of *The Fall*. However explicit the programming into the text may be, the reader I refer to remains, precisely for that reason, nothing more, or less, than what is best described as a textual construct.

I shall begin by considering the novel in the context of the other works of Camus that preceded it. *The Fall* is particularly disconcerting for those of its readers already familiar with the rest of the author's works. It is the only one of his works of fiction set in a gray, northern landscape, from which the sand, the sun, and the Mediterranean Sea are all absent. Nothing of Camus's earlier work can prepare the reader for Clamence's grating cynicism (with the possible exception of the character of Caligula, the hero of his play of the same name), nor for his profoundly pessimistic depiction of contemporary society. Here, contrary to the outcome of *The Stranger* or *The Plague*, there is no sign of light at the end of the tunnel, any glimmer of hope having been assiduously extinguished. In fact, *The Fall* can be seen to put seriously into question the whole of the author's previous literary output—the existentialism of *The Stranger* just as surely as the humanism of *The Plague*. Even the author of the former novel does not emerge unscathed, as is attested by the reference to "noble murderers" and "noble savages" (16; 23) noted earlier. Only by understanding the circumstances in which *The Fall* was conceived can we account for such an ostensibly un-Camusian work having come to be written by its author.

110

One of the crucial moments in the novel comes in the last chapter when the judge-penitent's companion reacts by laughing. The manner in the laugh is interpreted may well prove to be a determining factor in the way the reader's attitude to Clamence subsequently evolves. If, as suggested in the previous chapter, particular significance is not attached to the laugh and it is not taken as a sign of the listener's determination to resist Clamence's blandishments and entreaties, then neither will the protagonist's protestations that he is happy appear forced and unconvincing. Even the speaker's explicit reference to his companion being himself a Parisian lawyer (107; 155), coming as it does in the closing paragraph of the novel, is unlikely to undo or even attenuate in any way the impact of the judge-penitent's revelation of what he has been working toward from the outset. By this time, thanks to our sympathy for the speaker's professed predicament, we have already edged ourselves into the seat the unseen listener occupies—not, however, let it be stressed once again, because we necessarily identify as such with the listener, for we see ourselves in the same position relative to the speaker without necessarily sharing those few personal attributes of his addressee that have been made known to us.

The reader may well react in an utterly different manner, feeling sure that the judge-penitent has failed completely in his efforts to win over his listener. His insistence on his present happiness can as well be understood as proof of his desperation as he vainly claims, time and again, that his listener cannot fail to end up confessing to the very foibles Clamence enumerates throughout the monologue. In this case, the reader is inclined to stand back from the fictional character of the judge-penitent, contemplating him and his dilemma from a comfortable distance. Such a distance will not, however, necessarily imply emotional detachment. On the contrary, the reader may well feel moved by his desperate efforts to break out of the anguished solitude he has brought upon himself by his incessant soul-searching and introspection. It is here that the character's full potential as a tragic hero comes to the fore. The better we have come to understand him as a person—or, rather, the better we believe we have done so—the more we shall feel moved by his tortured monologue. There is much to be learned from this tale, whether it be the ever-present dangers of totalitarianism in its multifarious guises, the debilitating power of excessive introspection, or the need for human charity and understanding not only in our dealings with our fellows but also in our attitude toward ourselves if we are to attain that most difficult of human objectives, self-acceptance. Without a doubt, *The Fall* is also, among so many other things, a cautionary tale, a moral fable for the times we live in and the people we have become. Its force and effectiveness as such should not be underestimated, as it accounts for so much of its lasting impact upon its readers.

This moral dimension of the work will not, in all probability, be affected by the gender of the reader. If its appreciation calls for our understanding of the tragic flaws in the protagonist's character, the flaws in question are surely universal ones. Moreover, the contemplation of the character in his tragic predicament implies a certain distancing effect and does not entail our merging with the fictional character through a process of empathatic identification. What, however, of our account of a very particular form of implied reader in the previous chapter? What effect, if any, will the fact that *The Fall*'s actual reader may well happen to be a woman have on the process we analyzed in such detail?

There is no doubt that the addressee of the monologue is a man. Nor is there any doubt—although this fact is perhaps less readily appreciated by the anglophone reader of the work's translation—that it would have been very difficult, if not impossible, for its author to have been able to devise a fictional character whose sex remained undefined. This difficulty arises from the very nature of the French language, in which adjectives and past participles always reflect the gender of the nouns qualified and the subjects of the verbs, respectively. This means that the novelist was virtually obliged to opt for either an explicitly male or female addressee.

The crux of the matter is that our very use of the term *addressee* is ambiguous in the present context, for the addressee we have just referred to is that of the judge-penitent's monologue. The latter is by no means synonymous with the text's actual addressee, the reader of *The Fall*. The fictional character whose words and presence are merely implied is nonetheless the explicit addressee here. There does, however, occur, as was noted earlier, a subtle shift between the implied fictional listener and a peculiar form of implied addressee-reader, one not so much built into the text as generated by the very fact of the fictional listener's presence being implied rather than portrayed. The emergence of this implied addressee-reader is, in large part, attributable to the potential ambiguity of the shifter, the second-person pronoun.

It is at this point that the gender of the actual reader comes into play. As we saw in the last chapter, the implied addressee-reader remains nonetheless distinct from the monologue's implied listener, to whom the former owes its existence. And I say "*its* existence" advisedly, for a textual construct such as this implied addressee-reader must, of necessity, be genderless. This is not true of the implied reader as defined by literary theorists, such as Wolfgang Iser[1] which is why I have coined the neologism *implied addressee-reader* to differentiate the latter from the former. In *The Fall*, all the textual indices that could serve to characterize an implied reader are in fact taken up by the task of creating an implied listener. What is not implied, in the sense of being programmed into the text, is that the actual reader identify with this unseen listener. The implied addressee-reader proves interchangeable with the implied listener only in the sense that he occupies the same position as the latter in relation to the speaker's monologue. In other words, they share the same addressee status. In the final analysis, then, it matters not whether the actual reader is a man or a woman, since the concept of the implied adressee-reader—no doubt peculiar to this particular novel—does not carry with it any sexual identity as such. This does not, of course, mean that a female reader will react in the same way to this work as a male reader but merely that the text will provide her with the same range of optional interpretations as it does the male reader. It is possible that the reader's gender will play a role in determining the interpretation chosen and probable that it will have its part to play with regard to the precise nature of the reactions provoked within a given interpretive strategy.

Not all readers will be inclined to view the judge-penitent as a tragic figure, however. It is quite possible to consider his verbal delirium with all its excesses and exaggerations as somewhat comical. He then becomes a rather pathetic, even pitiful character for whom we may feel sorry but not one who will move us. To see this character as a kind of histrionic buffoon does not appear to be the most likely outcome of reading *The Fall*. It does, nevertheless, remain a possibility that cannot be passed over without acknowledgment.

This image of a grotesque and melodramatic Dostoevskian figure leads us into yet another radically different interpretation of this complex novel. It will no doubt prove to be the most unexpected interpretation, since it has barely been broached by other critics writing on *The Fall*.[2] For all that, it is by no means an arbitrary reading of the novel. This interpretation is founded on the marked analogy between this work and the theatrical genre. What if *The Fall* were, as virtually all its formal properties as a text suggest, a dramatic monologue in the strict sense of the term? The second and final dramatic revelation in the very last paragraph of the book whereby we learn that the unheard listener is himself a Parisian lawyer prompts this quite different reading of the judge-penitent's situation. Could it not be that the person to whom he has been talking all this time is no stranger but his own self-image as he looks into a mirror? It is certainly not easy to see any other raison d'être for this striking detail to have been introduced by the author so unexpectedly right at the end of the judge-penitent's monologue, although it is possible to attribute it to the general sense of irony running through the text. It might even be seen to suggest that the judge-penitent's companion is that much more likely to succumb to the temptation to embark upon his own confession, given his professional kinship with the speaker. But then again, the leitmotiv of the mirror, along with the mirror image of the double in particular, appears throughout the text. We actually witness his looking into the mirror when he remarks that his smile is double (31; 44). Moreover, his assiduous and methodical pursuit of the practice of introspection must of necessity have already accustomed him to talking to himself, as is revealed by his remarks in the very first chapter: "I walk for nights on end, I dream or *talk to myself interminably*" (11; 16; my emphasis). Also, Camus had himself toyed with the idea of staging *The Fall* in a Parisian theater and had in fact begun working on the text.

It is perhaps significant in this respect that the portraits of Clamence and his interlocutor do not reveal themselves to be mutually exclusive; they could in fact be seen to be interdependent, as is pointed out by Xavier Bonnier. Whereas Clamence describes his own physical features when he says, "By my stature, my shoulders, and this face that I have often been told was shy, I look rather like a football player" (9; 14), he creates only a general impression of his interlocutor: "You are my age in a way, with the sophisticated eye of the man in his forties who has seen everything, in a way" (9; 12–13). When he does mention his companion's physical appearance, he says, "You are well dressed in a way, that is as people are in our country; and your hands are smooth. Hence a bourgeois, in a way!" (9; 13), but his description is in keeping with his later portrayal of himself, with his "good manners . . . and fine speech" and "nails . . . manicured" (9; 14). Moreover, his own "fine speech" is in keeping with his interlocutor's appreciation, as a "cultured bourgeois," of the refined subjunctive tense of the verb. It is less obvious, however, whether the fact that "the camel that provided the hair for [his] overcoat may have been mangy" (9; 14) is compatible with his remark that his interlocutor is "well dressed in a way," although he does qualify the latter statement by adding, "That is as people are in our country" (9; 13).

The idea of ourselves as readers having witnessed nothing more than a lonely and desperate figure talking to himself as he scrutinizes his image in the mirror, seeking in this typical yet paradoxical fashion an answer to his dilemma, is an attractive one. It would then be in the very last paragraph of the novel—in a manner almost identical to the revelation at the end of *The Plague* that Rieux has been its narrator—that Camus would have turned the tables on his reader. The revelation of the other's profession as a lawyer would certainly be at the expense of the reader and thus complement that previous revelation of his motives and strategy as judge-penitent that had appeared to turn the tables on his unseen companion. The fact that his companion has remained unseen throughout the telling of his tale would itself receive the ultimate justification. What more fitting an image of the absurdity of the human condition than that of a man talking to his own image?

Indeed, we should note that to illustrate the absurd, the author evoked a comparable image in *The Myth of Sisyphus*, that of a man observed apparently talking to nobody but himself in a telephone booth (*Essais*, 108). Here again, the tragic dimension of the judge-penitent and his situation would be highlighted and it could not fail to move us.

This interpretation would carry with it a definite shift in the narrative situation. There would no longer be the kind of split addressee in the form of an implied listener and an implied addressee-reader, both being the creation not of the fictional character of the judge-penitent but of the author. The implied listener would be nothing but the creation of the protagonist, for not only would he continue to be conjured up solely by the words of the monologue but he would only exist in the imagination of its speaker. Moreover, the implicit addressee-reader would be erased from the text, since our view of the judge-penitent addressing his own image in the mirror would remove all possible ambiguity with regard to the identity of the second-person pronoun, just as the implied listener will have been banished from the scene of the fiction.

Such an interpretation, while not appearing to be necessarily far-fetched or implausible, since it finds definite textual confirmation, is not, however, in my view, the most likely one, as is confirmed by the main body of critical writings on this novel. I will therefore return to the very first interpretive scenario where the unseen listener is believed to be convinced by the judge-penitent and explore further its outcome and consequences for the reader. This reading of the novel has the advantage of respecting the formal workings of the text as analyzed in chapter 9, for the whole text has been seen, in the preceding chapters of this study, to be working toward such an end. It must be emphasized once again, however, that the text leaves us free to take the opposite view of the judge-penitent's success. Nonetheless, it is fair to claim, in the words of one critic (Jones, 76), that "whether Clamence's argument is accepted or rejected, it reverberates beyond the spoken or written text, demanding reaction."

In this reading of the work, we receive the full impact of the stranger's accusations. It is we ourselves, as readers, who bear the brunt of their force, for, on the one hand, the implied listener has proved to be too shadowy a figure (literally too insubstantial) to come between us and the judge-penitent's accusing finger and, on the other hand, the judge-penitent, having shed the mask of Jean-Baptiste Clamence, has become a wholly unknown quantity. That being so, what exactly remains for us to interpret?

If the world of the fiction has disappeared into thin air, having no more substance than the words that created the mirage, and if we know not to whom the accusatory finger belongs, there is no potential object of interpretation. If the speaker has consistently lied and there is no way of deciding whether he has uttered a single word that is not a falsehood, then it is not even possible to attempt to interpret the motivation for his lying. The identity of judge-penitent then becomes reduced to a verbal strategy or tactic devoid of any specified psychological motivation, because the motivation the speaker attributes to himself can no more be taken at face value than anything else he tells us. In other words, the role of judge-penitent may well be no less of a mask than the one he has just discarded, that of a certain Jean-Baptiste Clamence.

The world of the work has thereby become reduced to something decidedly less than a world, to the incitation to confess. But confess to what exactly? That is for us to decide individually.

There is here an incipient circularity in that we are, in a sense, called upon to utter again the same words we have mouthed silently through our reading of the novel, but with the radical difference that this time round, we shall be speaking in our own name. I noted earlier (in chapter 6) that the speaker indulges in a reinterpretation of his past life and thus mirrors the very activity the reader is involved in while reading Clamence's interpretation of past experiences, given that the reader is necessarily and simultaneously forming an interpretation of the novel—in short, an interpretation of an interpretation. It is as though the fictional character were anticipating the activity the reader will later be called upon to undertake in relation to his or her own existence, even if he himself is perhaps only going through the motions of interpreting; indeed, if that is the case, it is even more true to claim that

Clamence is showing the way to the reader in both senses of the expression: that is, both leading the way and modeling what has to be done.

The author thereby creates an ingenious textual device to entrap the reader. Through the very process of reading, we have already unwittingly prepared the ground for the task that we are forced to undertake: that of assuming for ourselves the reinterpretation of a past life and the resulting confession, both simulated by the monologue we have been silently articulating. Reading and speaking, rehearsing and repeating are processes that have become inextricably intertwined in what can, in the final analysis, be seen to be the paradigm of literary appropriation by readers, the process by which we come to terms with a work to make it our own.

In this strange way, the reader, as I suggested at the end of the previous chapter, becomes part of the problem posed by the interpretation of *The Fall* (Fitch, 1982, 69–88). The outcome of this reading of the novel is such that the reader finds himself or herself thrown back upon himself or herself, for the reader, in the form of his or her own life, is all that remains to be interpreted. Our natural desire and need to interpret, inseparable from the reading of any fiction, has but our own existence to feed upon. This means, in short, that literary aesthetics have been superseded by moral self-interpretation and hence evaluation. All the alternative readings of this novel cited earlier are, in my view, undercut by such an outcome.

In spite of what has just been said, the process involved here remains a literary one. It is none other than that of the appropriation by the reader of the literary work, for all literature that is adequately crafted by its author has its effect upon the reader, who takes away from the reading a conception of reality different from the one brought to bear on the given text. The renewed view of life that the reader now assumes is not, however, that of the work. Rather, the work has become transmuted into something else again by coming into contact with the reader's horizon of lived experience. The change brought about in the reader is the result of the ever-shifting adaptation by which two conceptions of reality—that of the work and that of the reader—come to terms with, and seek to accommodate, one another. By finally turning all its attention to the actual reader, as opposed to that implied reader contained within the confines of the text, *The Fall* awakens in its reader a heightened awareness of the process involved in the reading of any novel worthy of the name. It highlights the very interface between literature and reality by reducing itself, as its very world dissolves before the reader's bemused eye, to its impact on its reader: product has yielded to process. In the final analysis, this work speaks to the question not only of the nature of fictionality in its various guises but also to the relationship between literature and life. What it tells us is that the meaningfulness of that relationship lies not in the fact that literature depicts reality but that it plays a crucial part in determining the nature of that reality, for what we take away from our reading will serve to reshape our world.

11

Conclusion

The Fall is an unsettling work capable of profoundly disturbing its reader. It is not a book one can lay down, having finished reading it, and simply walk away from. Like that other great work of twentieth-century French fiction, Samuel Beckett's *L'Innommable* (*The Unnamable*), it has both an immediate and lasting impact upon its reader, who cannot emerge unscathed from the experience. Unlike the Beckett work, however, it is clearly designed to unsettle and disturb. It is not until its very last pages that the full import of its title is brought home to us and that we come to realize that its aim has been nothing less than to engineer the "fall" of its reader. And it is in his or her own eyes that the fall from grace has occurred with the impression of having "lost track of the light, the mornings, the holy innocence of those who forgive themselves" (106; 153).

In a sense, it is true that all Camus's fiction unsettles and disturbs the reader inasmuch as all three of his novels perturb and disrupt the relationship between the reader and the text, for there is something distinctly disconcerting about all three narrative voices. The reader does not know what to make of any one of them—Meursault's, Rieux's, or Clamence's—and has difficulty understanding why they speak as they do and grasping the psychological makeup underlying their tone of voice. The tale that each is telling somehow does not fit with the manner of its telling. *The Fall* goes further in this respect than its two precursors, for the various doubts and uncertainties that the narrative tone of voice raises in the mind of the reader not only remain unresolved by the end of the novel but become more explicit and distinctly more pressing. Having been intrigued and curious as to what Clamence was driving at and hence being unsure of the underlying motivation for his monologue, the reader now finds that he or she has become the object of those doubts, unsure of the possibility of surviving the rigors of such a merciless self-interrogation. If, as Clamence points out, our fellow humans are there to precipitate the Day of Judgment, once the seed of self-doubt has been sown and the judge and the judged have become synonymous, every day becomes a day of judgment.

The transformation of the reader-text relationship is also a characteristic of the French *Nouveau Roman* (New Novel), and it should not be forgotten that *The Fall* was published during a period that also saw the appearance not only of Beckett's trilogy but also of the first novels of Alain Robbe-Grillet and Michel Butor. In Camus's last novel, too, it is the formal properties of the text that are responsible for bringing about this transformation, but *The Fall* is remarkably innovative, for its creator has devised a narrative form that in the manner of its interaction with the reader, doubtless knows no precedent. There is here, however, a fundamental distinction to be made, for if the reader of the New Novel is invariably called upon to play a more active part by exchanging the role traditionally required of the reader with that of the novelist, *The Fall*'s reader becomes implicated in the reading on an existential level, as a human being with a past, present, and future that have nothing to do with aesthetics and everything to do with life as it is led.

In spite of its innovative formal characteristics, *The Fall* has in fact more in common with the writings of the French *moralistes* than with the French New Novel. Camus himself had denied, in his last interview before his death (*Essais*, 1927), any connection between *The Fall* and the exploratory writings of the New Novelists and stressed the influence of the theater. La Rochefoucauld's *Maxims* cannot fail to come to mind and even La Bruyère's *Caractères* (*Characters*) are not that far removed from Clamence's thumbnail sketches of his contemporaries and their lifestyles. Reading *The Fall*, one comes, perhaps for the first time, to appreciate why Camus considered himself a *moraliste* rather than a philosopher, for this work constitutes a veritable inventory of the foibles of modern man and a merciless account of the society they have given rise to.

There can be little doubt that *The Fall* represents Camus's finest achievement as a writer, and it could not have been more fitting that the very year after its publication, he was awarded the Nobel Prize. It is a work of humor, poetry, psychological complexity, and profound moral import. In a very real sense, this novel represents the confluence of a life and a work, of a creator and his creation, through a process of artistic alchemy whereby a brave new world comes into focus with an immediacy that holds our fascinated gaze. It is a vision that perfectly characterizes what Nathalie Sarraute referred to, in the title of a book of essays that appeared in the same year as *The Fall*, as "the age of suspicion."

Notes and References

Chapter One

1. The information in the present chapter is based on the most authoritative source available at present: Herbert R. Lottman, *Albert Camus: A Biography* (New York: Doubleday, 1979).

Chapter Two

1. René Girard ("Camus' Stranger Retried," *PMLA* 79, no. 5 [December 1964]) shows how *The Fall* puts Camus's first published novel into question, and David Ellison ("*The Fall*," in *Understanding Camus* [Columbia: University of South Carolina Press, 1990], 139–64) sees in it "a conscious and studied reversal of the values Camus had sought to define in his philosophical treatise" (142), *The Rebel*.

2. Although it was to be followed, a year later by his short-story collection *The Exile and the Kingdom*, a story such as "The Renegade" did nothing to reassure his readers. The drafts of the novel he was working on at his death, to be called "Le Premier Homme," have recently been published (cf. Le Premier Homme [Paris: Galliamard, 1994]).

3. Brian T. Fitch, "*L'Étranger*" *de Camus: Un Texte, ses lecteurs, leurs lectures* (Paris: Larousse, 1972).

4. "Albert Camus Reading in French *La Peste, La Chute, L'Été, L'Étranger*," Caedmon Records, New York, TC1138, 1960.

Chapter Three

1. Myrna Magnan-Shardt, "*La Chute* comme *skaz* une hypothèse génétique," *Albert Camus*, no. 6, "Camus nouvelliste: *L'Exil et le royaume*," 1973, 145–65.

2. Gaëtan Picon, "Mercuriale: Les Lettres: *La Chute* d'Albert Camus," *Mercure de France* 1116 (August 1956): 453–57.

3. Adele King, "Structure and Meaning in *La Chute*," *PMLA* 77, no. 5 (December 1962): 660–67. This article provided the basis for the chapter on *The Fall* in her book-length study *Camus*, 81–94 (Edinburgh: Oliver and Boyd, 1964).

4. Conor Cruise O'Brien, *Camus* (London: Fontana/Collins, 1970), 76–83.

5. Carina Gadourek, "Les Traîtres en enfer," in *Les Innocents et les coupables: Essai d'exégèse de l'œuvre d'Albert Camus* (The Hague: Mouton, 1963), 175–201.

6. H. Allen Whartenby, "The Interlocutor in *La Chute*: A Key to Its Meaning," *PMLA* 83, no. 5 (October 1968): 1326–33.

7. José Barchilon, "*The Fall* by Albert Camus: A Psychoanalytical Study," *International Journal of Psycho-analysis* 49 (1968): 386–89.

8. Michael A. Sperber, "Camus' *The Fall*: The Icarus Complex," *American Imago* 26, no. 3 (Fall 1969): 281–90.

9. Alain Costes, *Albert Camus ou la parole manquante* (Paris: Payot, 1973).

10. Jean Gassin, *L'Univers symbolique d'Albert Camus: Essai d'interprétation psychanalytique* (Paris: Librairie Minard, 1981).

11. Pierre-Louis Rey, *Camus: "La Chute"* (Paris: Hatier, 1970).

12. Brian T. Fitch, ed., *Albert Camus*, no. 3, "Sur *La Chute*" (1970).

13. Raymond Gay-Crosier ed. *Camus 1970: Colloque organisé sous les auspices du Département des Langues et Littératures romanes de l'Université de Floride* (Sherbrooke, Quebec: CELEF, 1970).

14. Roger Quilliot, "Clamence et son masque," in Fitch (1970), 83–100.

15. Brian T. Fitch, "Une Voix qui se parle, qui nous parle, que nous parlons, ou l'espace théâtral de *La Chute*," in ibid., 59–79.

16. Jacqueline Lévi-Valensi, "*La Chute*, ou la parole en procès," in ibid., 33–57.

17. André Abbou, "Les Structures superficielles du discours dans *La Chute*: Essai d'analyse des formes linguistiques," in ibid., 101–25.

18. Brian T. Fitch, "Clamence en chute libre: La Coherence imaginaire de *La Chute*," in Gay-Crosier, *Camus 1970*, 49–68.

19. Marten Nøjgaard, "Temps et espace dans *La Chute* de Camus: L'Importance des faits linguistiques comme signaux physiques de la structuration littéraire," *Orbis Litterarum* 26, no. 4 (1971): 291–320.

20. Claudine Maillard and Michel Maillard, *Le Langage en procès: Structures et symboles dans "La Chute" de Camus* (Grenoble: Presses Universitaires de Grenoble, 1977).

21. Brian T. Fitch, "Locuteur, délocuteur et allocutaire dans *La Chute* de Camus," in *L'Analyse du discours/Discourse Analysis*, ed. Pierre R. Leon and Henri Mitterand (Montreal: Centre Educatif et Culturel, 1976), 123–31.

22. Phan Thi Ngoc-Mai and Pierre Nguyen Van-Huy, with the collaboration of Jean-René Peltier, *"La Chute" de Camus, ou le dernier testament: Étude du message camusien de responsabilité et d'authenticité selon "La Chute"* (Neuchâtel: Éditions de la Baconnière, 1974).

23. As John J. Lakich had already done in "Tragedy and Satanism in Camus' *La Chute*," *Symposium* 24, no. 3 (Fall 1970): 262–76.

24. Marthe La Vallée-Williams, "Biblical Allusions in *La Chute*," *Agora* 2, no. 2 (Fall 1973): 13–31.

25. Jeffrey Meyers, "Camus' *The Fall* and Van Eyck's *The Adoration of the Lamb*," *Mosaic* 7, no. 3 (1974): 43–51.

26. Phillip H. Rhein, "The Northern Desert: A Comparison of Camus' *The Fall* and Van Eyck's *Ghent Altarpiece*," in *Albert Camus' Literary Milieu: Arid Lands: Proceedings of the Comparative Literature Symposium* (Lubbock: Texas Tech University Press, 1976), 151–66.

27. Jean Gassin, "*La Chute* et le retable de l' 'Agneau mystique': Étude de structure," in *Albert Camus 1980*, ed. Raymond Gay-Crosier (Gainesville: University Presses of Florida, 1981), 132–41.

28. Yves Reuter, *Texte/Idéologie dans "La Chute" de Camus* (Paris: Lettres Modernes, 1980).

29. François Zumbiehl, "Clamence et la perversité de la culture," *Acta Litteraria Academiae Scientarum Hungaricae* 17, nos. 3–4 (1975): 393–402.

30. Rosemarie Jones, *"L'Étranger" and "La Chute"* (London: Grant and Cutler, 1980).

31. David R. Ellison, "*The Fall*," in *Understanding Albert Camus* (Columbia: University of South Carolina Press, 1990), 139–64.

32. Alex Argyros, *Crimes of Narration: Camus' "La Chute"* (Toronto: Éditions Paratexte, 1985).

33. Evelyn H. Zepp, "Self and Other: Identity as Dialogical Confrontation in *La Chute*," *Perspectives on Contemporary Literature* 12 (1986): 51–56.

34. Èlaine Cliche, "Langage du pouvoir, pouvoir du langage, ou la narration à la première personne dans *La Chute* d'Albert Camus," *Revue de l'Université d'Ottawa* 54, no. 4 (October-December 1983): 15–24.

35. Brian T. Fitch, "The Interpreter Interpreted: *La Chute*," in *The Narcissistic Text: A Reading of Camus' Fiction* (Toronto: University of Toronto Press, 1982), 69–88.

36. Brian T. Fitch, "The Empty Referent: Camus' *La Chute*," in *Reflections in the Mind's Eye: Reference and Its Problematization in Twentieth-Century French Fiction* (Toronto: University of Toronto Press, 1991), 114–36.

37. Brian T. Fitch, "Le Paradigme herméneutique chez Camus," in *Albert Camus 1980*, 32–48, and "The Interpreter Interpreted."

38. Brian T. Fitch, "The Empty Referent."

39. David R. Ellison, "Vertiginous Storytelling: Camus's *La Chute*, 1956," in *Of Words and the World: Referential Anxiety in Contemporary French Fiction* (Princeton, N.J.: Princeton University Press, 1993), 27.

40. Maurice Blanchot, "*La Chute*: La Fuite," in *L'Amitié* (Paris: Gallimard, 1971), 228–35.

41. John Mowitt, *Text: The Genealogy of an Antidisciplinary Object* (Durham: Duke University Press, 1992).

Chapter Four

1. Jean-Claude Brisville, *Camus* (Paris: Gallimard, 1959), 241.

2. Carl A. Viggiani, "Notes pour le futur biographe d'Albert Camus," in *Albert Camus*, no. 1, "Autour de *L'Étranger*" (1968), 206.

3. *Carnets: 1942–1945* (Paris: Gallimard, 1962–64).

4. Simone de Beauvoir, *La force des choses* (Paris: Gallimard, 1963), 372.

5. Francis Jeanson, "Pour tout vous dire," *Les Temps modernes* 82 (August 1952): 339.

6. Ibid., 383.

7. Jean-Paul Sartre, "Réponse à Albert Camus," *Les Temps modernes* 82 (August 1952): 339 (Sartre's emphasis).

8. Ibid., 345.

9. Camus came explicitly to reject the epithet *existentialist*. Nonetheless, *The Stranger* and *The Myth of Sisyphus* have traditionally been considered to belong to the canon of existentialist literature.

10. Jean-Paul Sartre, "Explication de *L'Étranger*," in *Situations I* (Paris: Gallimard, 1947), 99–121 (first published in *Cahiers du sud*, February 1943).

Chapter Five

1. See Fitch, "Clamence en chute libre," and chapter 7.

Chapter Six

1. All italics in the quotations are Camus's unless otherwise indicated.

2. To draw out the full implications of this situation would be to reveal *The Fall*'s autoreflexivity as a text and produce a formalistic reading of it (Fitch, 1982, 69–88), which is not our concern here. See also Ellison (1993).

3. Camus's own attitude toward Christians is to be found in "L'Incroyant et les chrétiens" (*Essais*, 371–75).

4. Sandy Petrey, "The Function of Christian Imagery in *La Chute*," *Texas Studies in Language and Literature* 11, no. 4 (Winter 1970): 1445–54; R. P. Jacques Goldstain, "Camus et la Bible," in Brian T. Fitch, ed., *Albert Camus*, no. 4, "Sources et influences" (1971): 97–140.

Chapter Seven

1. An asterisk next to a page reference indicates that I had to modify the published translation in order for it more accurately to reflect the original French for the reasons just mentioned.

2. For a more detailed account of this imagery, see Fitch, "Clamence en chute libre."

Chapter Nine

1. In the next chapter, I shall consider the particular consequences of the reader's being a woman.

2. See Fitch, "Une Voix qui se parle."

Chapter Ten

1. Wolfgang Iser, *The Implied Reader: Patterns of Communication in Prose Fiction from Bunyan to Beckett* (Baltimore: Johns Hopkins University Press, 1974).

2. See Fitch, review of Rey's *Camus: "La Chute,"* in *Albert Camus*, no. 4 (1971): 235–36, and Jones, 74. However, more recently, Xavier Bonnier made a strong case for such a reading of the novel in "Clamence ou le soliloque absolu," *Poetique* 91 (September 1992): 299–313.

Bibliography

The reader is referred to the reviews of Camus criticism in the series *Albert Camus* (cited thus below), an irregularly published journal series entirely in French, issued by *La Revue des lettres modernes*. From 1968 to 1985 it was edited by Brian T. Fitch, and since 1986, by Raymond Gay-Crosier.

Primary Sources

Carnets (Notebooks) 1942–1945. Paris: Gallimard, 1962–1964. Translated by Philip Thody. London: Hamish Hamilton, 1966.

La Chute (The Fall). Paris: Gallimard, "Folio" 1972 (1st ed., Gallimard, 1956). Translated by Justin O'Brien. London: Penguin Books in association with Hamish Hamilton, 1963 (1st ed., Hamish Hamilton, 1957).

Essais (Essays). Edited by Roger Quilliot and L. Faucon. Paris: Gallimard, 1967.

La Peste (The Plague). Paris: Gallimard, "Folio" 1972 (1st ed., Gallimard, 1947). Translated by Stuart Gilbert. Harmondsworth, Middlesex: Penguin Books, 1960 (1st ed., 1948).

Secondary Sources

Biographies of Camus

Lottman, Herbert R. *Albert Camus: A Biography*. New York: Doubleday, 1979.

Viggiani, Carl A. "Notes pour le futur biographe d'Albert Camus." In *Albert Camus*, no. 1, "Autour de *L'Étranger*" (1968), 200–18.

Books on *The Fall*

Argyros, Alex. *Crimes of Narration: Camus' "La Chute."* Toronto: Éditions Paratexte, 1985.

Fitch, Brian T., ed. *Albert Camus*, no. 3, "Sur *La Chute*" (1970).

Gay-Crosier, Raymond, ed. *Albert Camus*, no.15, "Textes, intertextes, cortectes: Autour de *La Chute* (1994).

Jones, Rosemarie. *"L'Étranger" and "La Chute."* London: Grant & Cutler, 1980.

Maillard, Claudine, and Maillard, Michel. *Le Langage en procès: Structures et symboles dans "La Chute" de Camus*. Grenoble: Presses Universitaires de Grenoble, 1977.

Phan Thi Ngoc-Mai, and Nguyen Van-Huy, Pierre, with the collaboration of Jean-René Peltier. *"La Chute" de Camus ou le dernier testament: Étude du message camusien de responsabilité et d'authenticité selon "La Chute."* Neuchâtel: Éditions de la Baconnière, 1974.

Reuter, Yves. *Texte/Idéologie dans "La Chute" de Camus*. Paris: Lettres Modernes, 1980.

Rey, Pierre-Louis. *Camus: "La Chute."* Paris: Hatier, 1970.

Roston, Jacqueline Gabrielle. *Camus' récit "La Chute": A Rewriting through Dante's "Commedia."* New York: Peter Lang, 1985.

Sturm, Ernest. *Conscience et impuissance chez Dostoïevski et Camus: Parallèle entre "Le Sous-sol" et "La Chute."* Paris: Nizet, 1967.

Yadel, Martina. *"La Chute" von Albert Camus: Ansätze zu einer Interpretation*. Bonn: Bouvier, 1984.

Chapters in Books on *The Fall*

Ellison, David R. "*The Fall*." In *Understanding Albert Camus*, 139–64. Columbia: University of South Carolina Press, 1990.

———. "Vertiginous Storytelling: Camus's *La Chute*, 1956." In *Of Words and the World: Referential Anxiety in Contemporary French Fiction*, 25–43. Princeton, N.J.: Princeton University Press, 1993.

Bibliography

Fitch, Brian T. "The Interpreter Interpreted: *La Chute.*" In *The Narcissistic Text: A Reading of Camus' Fiction*, 69–88. Toronto: University of Toronto Press, 1982.

———. "The Empty Referent: Camus' *La Chute.*" In *Reflections in the Mind's Eye: Reference and Its Problematization in 20th-Century French Fiction*, 114–36. Toronto: University of Toronto Press, 1991.

Gadourek, Carina. "Les Traîtres en enfer." In *Les Innocents et les coupables: Essai d'exégèse de l'œuvre d'Albert Camus*, 175–201. The Hague: Mouton, 1963.

King, Adele. "*La Chute.*" In *Camus*, 81–94. Edinburgh: Oliver and Boyd, 1964.

Quilliot, Roger. "Un Monde ambigu." In *La Mer et les prisons: Essai sur Albert Camus*, 2d ed., 259–87. Paris: Gallimard, 1970.

Articles on *The Fall*

Abbou, André. "*La Chute* et ses lecteurs: Jusqu'en 1962." In *Albert Camus*, no. 3, "Sur *La Chute*" (1970): 9–19.

Blanchot, Maurice. "La Confession dédaigneuse." *La Nouvelle Revue Française* 48 (December 1956): 1050–56.

———. "*La Chute*: La Fuite." In *L'Amitié*. Paris: Gallimard, 1971.

Bonnier, Xavier. "Clamence ou le soliloque absolu." *Poétique* 91 (September 1992): 299–313.

Fitch, Brian T. "Clamence en chute libre: La Cohérence imaginaire de *La Chute.*" In *Camus 1970: Colloque organisé sous les auspices du Département des Langues et Littératures romanes de l'Université de Floride*, edited by Raymond Gay-Crosier, 49–68. Sherbrooke, Quebec: CELEF, 1970.

———. "*La Chute* et ses lecteurs: Depuis 1962." *Albert Camus*, no. 3, "Sur *La Chute*" (1970): 20–32.

———. "Une Voix qui se parle, qui nous parle, que nous parlons, ou l'espace théâtral de *La Chute*," *Albert Camus*, no. 3, "Sur *La Chute*" (1970): 59–79

———. "Locuteur, délocuteur et allocutaire dans *La Chute* de Camus." In *L'Analyse du discours/Discourse Analysis*, edited by Pierre R. Léon and Henri Mitterand, 123–31. Montreal: Centre Éducatif et Culturel, 1976.

Gassin, Jean. "*La Chute* et le retable de l''L'Agneau mystique': Étude de structure." In *Albert Camus 1980*, edited by Raymond Gay-Crosier, 132–41. Gainesville: University Presses of Florida, 1981.

Girard, René. "Camus' Stranger Retried." *PMLA* 79, no. 5 (December 1964): 519–33.

Goldstein, R. P. Jacques. "Camus et la Bible." *Albert Camus*, no. 4, "Sources et influences" (1971): 97–140.

Meyers, Jeffrey. "Camus' *The Fall* and Van Eyck's *The Adoration of the Lamb*." *Mosaic* 7, no. 3 (1974): 43–51.

Nøjgaard, Marten. "Temps et espace dans *La Chute* de Camus: L'Importance des faits linguistiques comme signaux physiques de la structuration littéraire." *Orbis Litterarum* 26, no. 4 (1971): 291–320.

Petrey, Sandy. "The Function of Christian Imagery in *La Chute*." *Texas Studies in Language and Literature*, 11, no. 4 (Winter 1970): 1445–54.

Whartenby, H. Allan. "The Interlocutor in *La Chute*: A Key to Its Meaning." *PMLA* 83, no. 5 (October 1968): 1326–33.

Zumbiehl, François. "Clamence et la perversité de la culture." *Acta Litteraria Academiae Scientiarum Hungaricae* 17, nos. 3–4 (1975): 393–402.

Index

Index

Quilliot, Roger, 17; *La Mer et les prisons* (*The Sea and Prisons*), 15; "Un Monde ambigu," 14

Religious dimension, 13, 17–18, 44, 54, 57–59
Reuter, Yves, 18, 19
La Revue des lettres modernes , 16
Rey, Pierre-Louis, 16
Rhein, Philip H., 17, 59
Ricoeur, Paul, 19
Robbe-Grillet, Alain, 121

Sadomasochism, 56
Sarraute, Nathalie, 122
Sartre, Jean-Paul, 17, 28; "L'Enfance d'un chef" ("The Childhood of a Leader"), 32; *L'Être et le néant* (*Being and Nothingness*), 32; *Huis clos* (*No Exit*), 30; *Les Mots* (*The Words*), 9; *La Nausée* (*Nausea*), 24; relationship with Camus, 3–4, 23–24, 27, 29, 32. *See also* Existentialism

Self-doubt, 105, 121
Sensuality, 26, 49
Shame, 31–32, 66
Sincerity, 47, 50, 52
Slavery. *See* Totalitarianism
Solitude, 66, 72
Sperber, Michael A., 16
Suicide, 86

La Table ronde, 4
Les Temps modernes, 28, 29, 33
Theater, imagery of, 106, 107
Totalitarianism, 54–56

UNESCO, 4

Van Eyck, Hubert: *The Adoration of the Lamb*, 17, 59
Van-Huy, Pierre Nguyen, 17

Whartenby, H. Allen, 16

Zumbiehl, François, 18

The Author

Brian T. Fitch is University Professor, University of Toronto; Gerald Larkin Professor of French, Trinity College; and a Fellow of the Royal Society of Canada. He was born in London and graduated from Kings College, Newcastle-upon-Tyne, in the University of Durham; he received a Doctorat d'Université from Strasbourg University. He is a founding coeditor of the journal *Texte* and past founding editor of the journal *Albert Camus* (1968–85). Among his numerous publications on Camus are *Narrateur et narration dans "L'Étranger" de Camus* (*Narrator and Narration in Camus's "The Stranger,"* [1960, 1968]), *Le Sentiment d'étrangeté chez Malraux, Sartre, Camus et S. de Beauvoir* (*The Feeling of Strangeness in the Works of Malraux, Sartre, Camus and S. de Beauvoir,* [1964, 1983]), *Essai de bibliographie des études en langue française consacrées à Albert Camus* (*A Bibliography of French-Language Studies Devoted to Albert Camus,* [1965, 1969, 1972]), *Un Texte, ses lecteurs, leurs lectures: Étude méthodologique de "L'Étranger" de Camus* (*A Text, Its Readers, Their Readings: A Methodological Study of Camus's "The Stranger,"* 1972), and *The Narcissistic Text: A Reading of Camus' Fiction* (1982). He has also written books on Malraux, Julien Green, Bernanos, Beckett, Bataille, and Blanchot.